COLLEGE
THE AMERICAN WAY

A Fun ESL Guide to English Language and
Campus Life in the U.S.

Sheila MacKechnie Murtha, M.A.
Jane Airey O'Connor, Ed.D.

Research & Education Association
Visit our website at: www.rea.com

Research & Education Association
258 Prospect Plains Road
Cranbury, New Jersey 08512
Email: info@rea.com

College the American Way: A Fun ESL Guide to English Language and Campus Life in the U.S.

Published 2019 by Research & Education Association, Inc.

Printed in the United States of America

Library of Congress Control Number 2016948505

ISBN-13: 978-0-7386-1213-3
ISBN-10: 0-7386-1213-8

Cover Image © iStockphoto.com/NLshop

Table of Contents

Part 5

Answers to Exercises

About Our Authors

(Everything you wanted to know . . . and more!)

Sheila and Jane have been colleagues and friends for . . . well, let's just say a long time. ☺ As ESL (English as a Second Language) teachers, they have worked together on tons of projects . . . and they always had lots of fun as they worked. A partnership was born!

Together, Jane and Sheila have teaching credentials in several states and on two continents. With years and years... and years... of experience (they just don't want to count them all, ha!), they have taught ESL to little kids, big kids, university students, adult workers, corporate executives, and other teachers in the U.S. and Europe (online and in regular classroom settings).

Sheila and Jane have served on the New Jersey Department of Education Advisory Committee for ESL/Bilingual Education. They've facilitated online ESL training courses for educators through the NJ DOE professional development program. Sheila has held several leadership positions scoring English teacher candidate responses for an international testing company, and Jane has written ESL test questions and rated English as a Foreign Language exams for another internationally recognized testing company. (They teach! They test! They score!)

Our authors have been recognized for excellence in teaching, and have been honored with several awards, including three Teacher-of-the-Year awards, as well as corporate citations for excellence. They've given numerous presentations, and they've written curricula and syllabi for diverse ESL populations. Add to this some fun teaching projects (French, Spanish, public speaking, drama, writing, and . . . no kidding . . . even soccer skills!) . . . and you've got two writers who know how to have a good time writing a book!

Jane is the founding Director of the ESL program at Emory College of Arts and Sciences in Atlanta, Georgia, where she has worked since 2007. She has rated ITA students at Princeton (with Sheila!), and taught at Burlington County College and Westampton Schools.

Sheila has been a Lecturer at the University of Pennsylvania English Language Program since 2007. As her family grew and moved, Sheila has always found a home in universities: rating ITA students at Princeton University (with Jane!); and teaching at universities north and south: William Paterson University, Rutgers University, and Francis Marion University.

Sheila and Jane may live several states apart, but they always find time to work together on FUN projects . . . like this book!

A Letter from the Authors

Hi there!

Thanks for choosing our book. We hope you'll love it!

You probably know from the other books in our *English the American Way*® series that we have lots of FUN writing for *you*. We hope *you* have lots of fun reading this, and our other books!

In this book, *College the American Way*, we've tried to answer all your *study in the U.S.* questions . . even before you think of them! Learn about college life, customs, culture, and . . . (our favorite ➜) FUN! Find tons of new vocabulary and idioms, with grammar notes (Language Spots) to keep you sharp. Read (and hear) plenty of informal English . . . as native speakers speak it!

Enjoy our book . . . but don't forget to do your homework, ha!

With our very best wishes,

Sheila   *Jane*

Authors' Acknowledgments

Sheila says: I am grateful to my parents, Peg and Russ MacKechnie, for... well, . . . *everything*; to Erin, James, and the forever-voice in my head and my heart... they *are* everything.

Special thanks to Mak Yu-Ching, whose brilliant ideas and insider perspective provided Eureka moments . . . and some of the best tips!

Jane says: To my family in the UK—I may be far away but you are ever present in my mind. I look forward to every trip to Old Blighty and I miss you every day when I am not there! To my much smaller (actually tiny) family in the USA—Tony and Charlotte, you both mean the world to me. To my entire family . . . Thank you for my past, my present and my future. I love you all very much!

Symbols Used in the Book:

ⓘ	Look for this symbol in the vocabulary lists to find informal words and phrases. Native English speakers use these every day, and our definitions will help you figure out exactly how *you* can use them in conversation too.
	THINK ABOUT IT sections let you compare your experiences and analyze your own thoughts and attitudes.
	Show your superpowers as you use the new language in fun **quizzes**!
	Okay, you've studied all that vocabulary . . . Now, **USE IT**!
	FUN stuff!
	Cool tips!
	ROAD TRIP! Fun places to go!

How This Book Works

The emphasis is on fun in this lighthearted guide to college culture and language in the United States.

College the American Way answers the *who? what? where? why?* and *how?* questions about studying in the U.S. Learn who can help, what to do, where to go, why to check out housing and meal plans, and how to . . . HAVE FUN! Each part of the book is full of vocabulary, informal language, idioms, phrasal verbs, dialogues, and activities.

Look for the **By the Way** boxes. They have little tips and explanations about stuff American students already know. The **Think About It** sections give you time to compare cultures and analyze your own thoughts.

Language Spots in every section give you lots of grammar and usage information. Then practice with the fun activity.

There are quizzes in every section for you to practice what you've learned. Look for: **Try It!, Your Turn!,** and **Use Your Words!** Each of these activities will help you *use* the culture and language information you've just read. Then listen to the dialogues to *hear* the language spoken by native English speakers.

You'll love the **Culture Catch-Up** section! There are jokes in **Just For Fun**, **Tips** about American culture, and fun things to see and do in **Road Trips**. Check out **Quick Facts** and **Any Questions?** for cool notes about American geography, history, and culture.

Good luck, and HAVE FUN!

About REA

Founded in 1959, Research & Education Association (REA) is dedicated to publishing the finest and most effective educational materials—including study guides and test preps—for students of all ages.

Today, REA's wide-ranging catalog is a leading resource for students, teachers, and other professionals. Visit *www.rea.com* to see a complete listing of all our titles.

Acknowledgments

In addition to our authors, we would like to thank Pam Weston, Publisher, for setting the quality standards for production integrity and managing the publication to completion; Larry B. Kling, Vice President, Editorial, for his direction; Diane Goldschmidt, Managing Editor, for project management; and Kathy Caratozzolo for typesetting this edition.

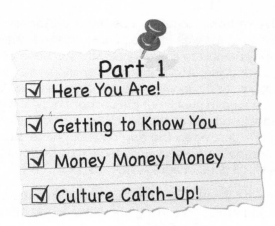

Part 1
- ☑ Here You Are!
- ☑ Getting to Know You
- ☑ Money Money Money
- ☑ Culture Catch-Up!

HERE YOU ARE!

Arriving in America

WOW! You did it! Can you believe it? **Go on**, give yourself a **pat on the back**—you **figured out** everything that had to be done . . . and YOU DID IT! You have the **applications**, **documents**, visas, forms, files—**phew**! You **filled in, filled out, signed on the dotted line** . . . That's **a lot of paperwork**! But . . . YOU DID IT! You figured out all the **red tape**, signed all the official documents, put your **initials** on changes to all the official documents, and now you're **finally** here!

Is someone meeting you at the airport? We hope you figured that out before you left, ha! If not, there are always ways to get where you need to go. Taking a **shuttle** is probably the easiest plan. Your **luggage** will **fit** easily, and the **van** will **drop you off right** at the door. **Door-to-door** service! But if you need a **Plan B**: Most airports have buses or trains that will take you into the city. That's easy if you don't have a lot of luggage; however, if you have **lots of** bags it can be **pretty tricky** getting on and off the train. Those **suitcases** are heavy, and they take up a lot of space! If you're lucky, the bus will have a **baggage compartment** . . . And if you're *really* lucky, the driver will help you **stow** your **stuff**!

A more **expensive option** is to take a **cab**. Most **major** airports have a **taxi stand**—a place where cabs wait to take people wherever they need to go. Sometimes you may be able to share a cab with someone who's going in the same direction you're going. And speaking of sharing—the popular **ride-share** services offer door-to-door service, usually at a much lower cost than a taxicab's **fare**. Be sure to check out the **carpool** option! If others are going in the same direction, you can share the cost of the ride, and the app will do all the planning work. Just **open the app** on your phone, **tap in** where you want to go, and someone will show up in a car to drive you to your door. No money needed—it's all done in-app. Away you go!

Yes, here you are—It's the place you've been dreaming about for so long! (Okay, so maybe you weren't dreaming about the *airport*, haha, but you know what we mean. . .) WELCOME to the U.S.!

THINK ABOUT IT

What's your **first reaction**? What's the first thing that you noticed? Was your **first impression** of the U.S. exactly what you **pictured** in your mind? Is this city bigger than you imagined? Smaller? More **crowded**? Louder? Busier? Have a great time exploring your new college home!

BY THE WAY . . .

We know—you just can't survive without that smartphone. In English, these are the magic words to say what you do on that phone:

- **open the app:** touch an icon to start using the program
- **tap:** touch the phone screen (on your computer we say *click*)
- **double tap:** touch twice, very quickly (on your computer we say *double click*)
- **press the home button:** touch the small button at the bottom (This "wakes up" your screen)
- **swipe:** move your finger across the screen
- **icon:** the little picture that represents the application (app)

LANGUAGE SPOT: BAGS

Wow. *Luggage*, *baggage*, *suitcases* and *bags* . . . they all refer to the same thing: the cases holding all that stuff you packed for your American study adventure! Yes, they refer to the same thing, but we don't use them **interchangeably**. *Luggage* and *baggage* are non-count nouns (sometimes called *uncountable*); *suitcase* and *bag* are count nouns (sometimes called *countable*).

- *Luggage* is a non-count noun. It's never used as a plural (with s). *Luggage* can refer to many bags, but it's used as one (collective) unit. So, your luggage *is* in the taxi (even if it means four bags!). And yes, it's used in the singular, but you do not use an article. If you buy too much stuff while you're here, you may need to buy *luggage* (or *some* luggage, but never *a* luggage) for the trip home!

- *Baggage* is also a non-count noun—never used in the plural. It usually refers to the suitcases (luggage!) that you load onto the plane or train. With a little luck (haha) your *baggage* won't get lost, and you'll find it at Baggage Claim when you arrive!

- *Suitcase* and *bag* refer to the individual items. They're count nouns, and you can use both in the singular (yes, use an article) and the plural. You may need to buy a *suitcase* before you return home. You may think three *suitcases* will be enough, but you may need another one for all the cool stuff you buy while you're here!

  The taxi driver can put two *bags* in the back seat; a *bag* will have to go in the front, next to him.

  Most airlines allow only one **carry-on** bag.

TRY IT!

Can you choose the correct *bags* word in the following sentences? Answers are on page 221.

1. Oh no! I've got too much _____ to fit in the car.

2. Exactly how many _____ do you have?

3. I've got four _____, but the airline's limit for checked (4.) _____ is three.

5. Well, at least you won't have to buy more _____ in the U.S.

6. I'm not so sure about that. If I can't fit all my new shoes into one _____ I'll have to buy more (7.) _____.

8. I really like your carry-on _____!

9. Thanks! I've always wanted to have a leather_____.

10. Well, I hope all my _____ shows up at Baggage Claim when I arrive at the airport!

DIALOGUE: AUDIO TRACK 2

We're Here . . . Now What?

HE: We did it! **I can't believe it**, but **we did it!** We're here! Take a look at that sign: "Welcome to the U.S.!" That's *us*! We're here in the *United States of America*. . .

SHE: I know! Just think: We'll be studying here for FOUR YEARS! We'll be **experts** at speaking English, ha! And we'll also have a **fancy** college **degree** when we're finished. But um, for right this minute. . . . Yeah, we're here . . . but . . . **now what**?

HE: Well, I don't know about you, but the first thing I want to do is **grab something to eat**. I'm **starving**! Let's get our bags at Baggage Claim and find someplace to get a nice American lunch.

SHE: Sounds good to me . . . I'm hungry too. But we haven't exchanged our **currency** yet—we don't have American money.

HE: No worries. We've got **plastic**!

SHE: Uh-oh. Will we be able to pay for a taxi with plastic?

HE: Sure, most cabs take credit cards. Or maybe we can just get an **Uber**. We'll be fine. I'm not worried about the cab. I'm worried about my stomach! I'm hungry—let's find someplace to eat!

SHE: Okay, okay. **Hey**, wait ... Look what I found at the bottom of my carry-on bag—a **twenty** from my visit last year! We can use that for lunch!

HE: Ha, twenty **bucks**?! That will never **cover** lunch AND a cab. . . . But hey, it's a good idea to **break** the twenty. Then we'll have some smaller **bills** for **tips**.

SHE: Great idea. I'll buy a magazine at the **newsstand** and get **change** for the twenty.

HE: Hmm, yeah. Maybe two fives, and the rest in singles? That should cover tips for lunch, and for all the bags too.

SHE: Too much luggage! I told you we should have **packed light**!

HE: What?! I *did* pack light! I only have one suitcase! All the other bags are yours!

SHE: Well, um, yes, but it's all *very* important stuff! Okay, let's go **pick up** the luggage and get something to eat!

YOUR TURN!

Can you answer these questions about the sections above? Answers are on page 221.

1. What phrase tells you he's really hungry? _____

2. How much American money did she find in her bag?

   _____

3. What expression does he use to mean "get smaller bills"?

   _____

4. What are "two fives"? _____

5. What phrase means *do not* bring a lot of stuff? _____

6. What expression means pick you up exactly where you are, and bring you to the entrance of where you want to go? _____

7. What is "plastic"? _____

8. What's the difference between a taxi and a cab? _____

9. What's the word for the small shop at an airport that sells newspapers, magazines, and small items? _____

10. What word means only the first letters of your first, middle, and last names? _____

BY THE WAY . . .

Tipping for services is expected in the U.S. If an airport worker helps with your bags, you should tip that person. The usual baggage-handling tip is $1 per bag. For other services, tips are usually 15% to 20%. The better the service the bigger the tip! (That includes taxi drivers. If the driver helps with your luggage, add $1 per bag. Hey, we told you not to pack so much **stuff**!)

VOCABULARY

- **a lot of:** many; much
- **application:** a form with personal information used to apply to a school or for a job
- **baggage compartment:** the place on a bus, train, or airplane where you put your bags
- **bills:** paper money
- **break** (a bill): exchange a large bill for smaller bills or coins
- ⓘ **bucks:** dollars
- **cab:** taxi
- **carpool:** people going to the same place sharing a ride in one car
- **carry-on:** a small bag (luggage!) that you can bring on the plane with you. Airlines are very strict about the size of a carry-on, so be sure to check the rules before you go to the airport!
- **change:** coins; also, get smaller bills and coins from a large bill; also, the money you get back after paying with a larger bill than the amount due
- **cover:** be enough to pay for something
- **crowded:** filled with TOO many people!
- **currency:** a country's money

- **degree:** The document that shows you've completed all the requirements for graduation in your program of studies. See how smart you are?
- **document:** official, important paper
- ⓘ **door-to-door:** from one exact place to another exact place
- ⓘ **drop someone off:** leave someone at a place
- **expensive option:** choice that costs more
- **expert:** person with special knowledge or skills
- ⓘ **fancy:** very special; impressive; often expensive
- **fare:** cost of the ride in a cab, bus, train, or airplane
- ⓘ **figure out :** analyze something to understand it
- ⓘ **fill in:** complete the individual items in a form with information
- ⓘ **fill out:** complete a form with information
- **finally:** at last! after a long time
- **first impression:** your first opinion
- **first reaction:** what you think right away; your first opinion
- **fit:** have enough room; be the right size
- **go on:** continue
- ⓘ **grab something to eat:** get something to eat
- ⓘ **hey!:** said to get someone's attention
- **I can't believe it:** I never thought it would happen!
- **icon:** the little picture that represents an application (app)
- **initials:** The first letters of your first, middle, and last names (Ours are SMM and JAO.)
- **interchangeably:** something able to be used in the place of another thing
- ⓘ **lots of:** many
- **luggage:** suitcases and/or bags; used in the singular form only
- **major:** large; important; also a student's main field of study in college
- **newsstand:** small shop to buy, ahem, NEWSpapers, magazines and snacks (Ha! Did somebody say SNACKS?)
- ⓘ **no worries:** "it's not a problem"; "it's okay"
- ⓘ **now what?:** What's the problem now?
- **open the app:** touch an icon to start using a program
- ⓘ **pack light:** don't put a lot of things in the bags
- **paperwork:** forms, reports, letters . . . any papers you need to complete
- ⓘ **pat on the back:** an acknowledgment that you did something well
- ⓘ **phew!:** word to express relief

- **pick up:** collect; lift off a surface; learn something informally
- **picture:** think about; imagine
- **Plan B:** what you'll do if your first plan doesn't work
- **plastic:** debit and credit cards
- **press:** push with a little force
- **pretty:** quite
- **red tape:** too many forms, papers, documents, applications to fill out, and too many rules to follow!
- **ride-share:** pay to ride in a person's private car (use that app!)
- **right:** exactly
- **shuttle:** small bus or train that goes to and from point A and point B
- **sign on the dotted line:** write your signature on a form
- **sounds good to me:** I think that's a good idea!
- **starving:** very hungry
- **stow:** store; put away
- **stuff:** things
- **suitcase:** a large bag, usually rectangular, used to carry clothes and other items while traveling
- **swipe:** move your finger across a screen
- **tap in:** enter information by touching the screen of the device
- **tap:** touch a phone screen
- **taxi:** cab
- **tip:** extra money you give for a service—for example, to a server in a restaurant
- **tricky:** difficult or challenging
- **a twenty:** a twenty dollar bill
- **Uber:** one of the most popular ride-share services
- **van:** a vehicle bigger than a car, smaller than a bus
- **we did it!:** we were successful! Yay!
- **WOW!:** word to express surprise or excitement

USE YOUR WORDS!

Unscramble to find the new word from the section above. Answers are on page 221.

1. _____ This is not how I <u>reupticd</u> the campus. It's much larger than I thought!

2. _____ The hardest part about coming to this college was filling out the lcpnoaipiat.

3. _____ Did somebody say "lunch"? I'm gsrtvnia!

4. _____Let's find a place to wost our luggage while we eat.

5. _____ Let's take the thulest to the mall. It's cheaper than a taxi.

6. _____ Hurry! Change your money into the local cyrucren so you can go shopping right away!

7. _____ This bag is so heavy! Okay, I admit it—I packed too much fufst.

8. _____ Phew! The airport was really ddwcore. It's nice to be out in the fresh air!

9. _____ I'm glad I bought this new ggguela. The bags are so easy to wheel.

10. _____ After four years of hard work (and a lot of fun!), you'll graduate with your eeedgr.

GETTING TO KNOW YOU

Welcome, New Students!

Orientation

Whew! You're here! **Bye-bye**, airport. **So long**, taxi. **See you later**, shuttle bus. Yes, you have arrived at your new home for the next few years. Welcome to **campus**! Your first stop will be to **check into** your **residence hall**. We hope you remembered to fill out that form—you know, the one where you requested the type of room you prefer. If not—haha, you may be sleeping on the classroom floor! Okay, we're only kidding about that, but admit it—it's pretty funny to think about.

We know you're tired from the long trip . . . but *TOO BAD!* There's no time for a **nap**! Take a quick look around your new room, put down your heavy luggage, and take a look at the schedule . . . It's time for . . . **ORIENTATION**! Yay!

We **get it**. You're tired. You're excited. (And if you're like us, you're HUNGRY!) You don't know anyone. You're probably a little nervous about what to do and where to go. But here's the **genius** part about orientation—the entire event is planned to help you with every one of those worries! (Yes, even the hungry part. We can almost taste those chocolate chip cookies, just thinking about them! **Yum**!) Oh yeah—and it will be FUN.

The orientation team has been planning for this all summer. **Faculty** and students have planned games and activities, and everyone is excited about meeting the new first-year students—YOU! In fact, everyone is so excited to share information with you that you may feel **overwhelmed** by the **tons** of stuff! You'll learn what fun things there are to do on campus and in the local community. The orientation team will give you information about: classes, clubs, campus **resources**, where to pay **tuition** bills, how to get money transfers wired to you from your family at home, how to change classes, and where to find the most popular food trucks (we think that's the most important information!). Food trucks! Ha, who needs student cafes? The **food trucks** have the best and cheapest food around campus!).

You get the idea. Tons of information!

As an international student, you'll probably have a special program before the main orientation for all new students. Yes, you're special! This special program will give you some time to get adjusted to the American campus and get over that **jet lag**! Students and faculty can answer any questions you have about documents, forms . . . and lunch! Someone may bring you to the offices where you'll get your student **ID** and make copies of important papers. Uh-oh. Did you forget to research the U.S. voltage system? Someone can tell you where to get an **adaptor** so you can plug in your appliances. (Or even better: They can tell you where to buy a new hair dryer here—some cost only about ten dollars!) You'll learn about **maintaining** your student visa and about the resources available to you as an international student. Your program will help you get all the **right** papers to all the right places!

But first, you'll really need that student ID. If you want to use any of the campus **amenities**, like the library or the copy center, you'll need to **show** your ID. You can't **sign up** for the gym unless you show your ID. (We know you can't wait to start exercising, ha!) Your college ID is very **handy** for other things too. A lot of places, like local restaurants, movie theaters, and bookstores will give students a **discount** if they show their ID. Many cultural and arts **venues** encourage young people to attend **exhibits**, concerts, and shows, so they offer **special pricing** with student ID. HEY! *We* want a student ID!

Many colleges have special **ESL** programs with English writing and other **tutoring** services. In these programs you'll be matched with a **tutor** who can help you with academic subjects that may be difficult for you. Make sure you **take advantage of** these free (!) resources for a successful year! This is a perfect time to meet other international students . . . even students from your home country. Yes, we know—it's exciting and fun to meet people from all over the world, and **OF COURSE** you'll want American friends . . . But we know that sometimes it's comforting to speak your own language, eat your own favorite foods, and just be with people from your own culture.

Wow! Does this sound like a lot to do? Are you tired just thinking about it? Relax! Actually, you've done a lot already! Remember those online activities you completed? The English proficiency tests you took? The forms you filled out for hours? You may even have taken placement tests for some of your classes. (These are to help schedule you for class levels where you'll feel most comfortable.)

Wasn't that special international student program fun? Do you think you can . . . *finally* . . . test your new mattress and . . . finally . . . have a NAP? Sorry—no! Now it's time for the main orientation, with all the other new students. Think about it this way: You've had some time to meet the other international students, and now it's time to make more American friends! Here's how it usually works: All the students will meet in one place, often a large **auditorium** or meeting room. The orientation team will introduce themselves, and each person will give a presentation. There may be tables around the room with **flyers** and **brochures** and applications and information about activities. (It's probably a good idea to bring a bag—you'll be collecting tons of papers that you can look over later.) Experienced students will be around to answer your questions and show you where to go. And here's the best part of orientation—**FREEBIES**! You'll get free pens, free **mugs**, free t-shirts, free bags . . . FREE STUFF! Some places we know even give the new students **stress balls**. . . **just in case**, ha! (But we're sure you won't need those.)

Once you've collected all the cool free stuff, you can choose to attend meetings about topics you want to know more about. For example, one session may discuss how you can **support** your academic studies. Another may give helpful information about services for students with disabilities. You can attend sessions about career paths you're interested in, like business, medicine, engineering, or design, among lots of others. There are sessions sponsored by different student organizations and religious organizations.

But we're not finished yet! You'll also have to attend some **mandatory** sessions, so make sure you look very carefully at the schedule. These may be meetings with your faculty advisor, or residence hall meetings to discuss life in the **dorms**. Best of all, there will be lots of social events scheduled to help you meet other students. Are you worried that you'll never remember everything you hear at orientation? Don't worry—you don't have to remember everything. You just have to remember where you put all the flyers!

And did we mention food? Oh boy, how could we forget to mention food? (Haha, by now you probably know that food is our favorite part of every activity!) Yes, food—there will be plenty of it! Everyone wants to welcome you with **delicious goodies**. Breakfast, **brunch**, **ice cream socials**, **boxed lunches**, **BBQs**, pizza parties, cookies and energy drinks . . . Uh-oh. This may be the start of the "**Freshman 15!**" (Hey, don't blame us . . . blame orientation.)

Yes, orientation is a crazy few days, but then it's time to **get down to business**, **enrolling** in classes and getting set for future success. Hmm, now where did you put all those flyers. . .?

THINK ABOUT IT

What was the hardest part about coming to the U.S.? Was it making the decision to study so far away? Was it saying good-bye to your family and friends? Was it ALL THE PAPERWORK and RED TAPE? Well, we can't help with the paperwork problem, but we *do* know that you'll soon be making lots of new friends.

BY THE WAY . . .

You love **fast food**! We love fast food! And now, welcome to the world of **take-out** and pizza! Although many students have become much more **sensible** about eating **nutritious** foods, college is still a time when lots of kids find it easier to **order out** and eat **junk food**. Can you guess what happens next? Ha—yes, you can! It's the dreaded "Freshman 15"! And what is that? you ask. We're sorry to tell you that it means the average number of pounds a first-year student **gains** at school. Watch out for that all-you-can-eat meal plan! Just because you can eat as much as you want doesn't mean you *should*. Hurry up—get that student ID and sign up for the gym!

LANGUAGE SPOT: INTERJECTIONS AND EXCLAMATIONS!

What the heck?! What's everyone getting so excited about? Well, we don't know what's so exciting, but it sure does sound like fun. Why? Because of . . . interjections and exclamations! These are words (interjections) or phrases (exclamations) used very commonly in informal speech. They express emotion in a fun way. (You've probably noticed that we love these expressions.) Interjections and exclamations can show surprise, or fear, or pain (Oh no! We hope it's not *our* pain!), or . . . just a sense of fun. You'll hear them all the time. They make speaking (and casual writing) more interesting, but *don't* plan to use these in your academic writing. *AAAAAAACK, NO!!!!!*

You can probably figure out what most interjections mean just by how they sound. For example, if someone says "Wow!" with a rising intonation, it's probably a very happy Wow! A falling intonation may mean someone is impressed . . . but not in a good way. Notice how these expressions are used, how they sound, and how people look when they say them, and we're sure you'll get the idea, but here's a little chart to help you along.

The Fun Words	Meaning	Example
Oh no! Aaack! Yikes!	This is very bad!	Oh no! I need to email my paper and the Internet is down! Aaack! The Internet is down again! Yikes! She wants us to complete that project in two days! I better get started!
Rats!	This is disappointing/terrible/very bad!	Rats! Everyone's going to the concert, but I have to finish my paper.
Wow! Man!	I'm impressed, amazed!	Wow! I can't believe there were so many people in Times Square on New Year's Eve!
Whew! Phew!	That was *almost* a big problem! What a relief!	Whew, we almost missed the train, but we got here just before the doors closed. The Internet is working again, so I can send my paper on time. Phew!
Eww! Ick! Ugh! Yuck.	That's disgusting!	Eww, there's a hair in my soup!
Uh-oh. Oops. Oopsie.	This is a problem. This is a little problem or mistake.	Uh-oh. I forgot to call my parents when I arrived. I hope they're not worried. Oops! I spilled my coffee on the new sofa. Rats! I forgot to wash my coffee cup this morning. Oopsie.
uh-huh	Yes.	"Oh, did you tell your Mom that you would call?" "Uh-huh."
uh-uh	No.	"So, did you call her?" "Uh-uh. I forgot."

The Fun Words	Meaning	Example
Uhh. . . Hmm. . . Umm. . .	I'm thinking. . ..	Uhh. . . I'm not sure I locked the door before I left. Hmm. . . I **wonder** if the bookstore is still open. Umm. . . I'm not sure I like banana broccoli ice cream!
Huh.	I didn't know that. That's surprising.	Huh, you were right about the time of the concert.
Huh?	What? Is that true?	Huh? We have a test this afternoon?
What the heck!? heck of a lot!	I'm surprised! I'm confused! What's going on? Wow, a LOT!	What the heck?! There's a huge crowd of people standing outside our dorm! At LotsOfBucks Coffee Shop today, my Mom said, "Eight bucks is a heck of a lot of money to pay for a small coffee!"
Ouch! Ouch.	That hurts! I feel sensitive about that.	Ouch! I bumped my head getting into the car. Ouch. You told me that my girlfriend has a new boyfriend.
Yay!	That's really great!	Yay, our team is winning the game!

TRY IT!

What expression might a speaker use in the following dialogue? More than one answer is possible! Yay! Answers are on page 222.

HE: (1) _____! I missed the last train. (2) _____ , I wonder how I'll get home.

SHE: (3)_____. Does your roommate have a car to come get you?

HE: (4)_____. We're both freshmen so we can't have cars on campus.

SHE: (5)_____! Take a look at this weekend schedule. That wasn't the last train you missed!

HE: (6)_____? Are you sure? A weekend schedule?

SHE: (7) _____. They just started it last month.

HE: (8)_____. This schedule says there's one more train in ten minutes. (9) _____, that's a relief!

SHE: (10)_____, you sure are lucky! Now you'll be able to finish your paper tonight!

DIALOGUE: AUDIO TRACK 3

A *Painting* Class?!

HE: Whew, I'm exhausted! Orientation was fun but it was a little overwhelming!

SHE: I know . . . so much information! But I feel a lot better now that I know there's so much extra help for us here. I didn't expect tutors, a Writing Center, and academic advisors. And best of all— it's FREE!

HE: I was so glad to meet my personal advisor. He's so friendly! And he gave me some really good information about what classes I should take. I told him I planned to take two writing classes and two math classes first **semester**, so the **required courses** are **out of the way**, but he told me that would be too much.

SHE: *Two* writing classes? AND two math classes? First semester? In English? What the heck were you thinking? *Of course* that's too much!

HE: Ha, yeah, that's what my advisor said. Well. . . what he actually said was, "ARE YOU CRAZY?!"

SHE: Haha! He sounds like a funny **guy**. So what did you finally decide?

HE: I decided not to be crazy. I'll take only one required first-year writing class, a math class, a biology class, the first-year **seminar** and . . . well, are you ready for this?... a painting class!

SHE: Wait, WHAT? A *painting* class? PAINTING?

HE: I get the feeling that you don't think I'm the next Picasso . . . But hey, you never know!

SHE: Um . . . I'm pretty sure I DO know . . . I've seen your "artwork" on our lunch napkins.

HE: Well, I may not be Picasso, but I think it will be fun to learn some painting techniques.

SHE: Great! When we get back home you can paint my mom's kitchen! HA!

HE: Oh, very funny. *Anyway* . . . My advisor said that I need to take some electives along with my required courses. Then later I'll concentrate on my professional courses. There are so many interesting **electives** . . . Hey, I may even take a DANCE class later!

SHE: HA! I can just picture you in a **tutu**!

HE: Hey, that reminds me of a joke: Why does a ballerina wear a tutu?

SHE: *Ummm . . .*

HE: Because a *oneone* is too small, and a *threethree* is too big.

SHE: *AAAAARGHHHHH!!!!!* I think it's time for us to forget the jokes, and go find one of those fabulous food trucks they were talking about.

HE: Ha! And after all the fabulous food from the **fabulous** food truck, I think we better find the fabulous gym!

YOUR TURN!

What do you remember from the previous sections? Write *True* or *False*. Answers are on page 222.

1. _____ Orientation is a time to learn about campus resources.

2. _____ All sessions at orientation are mandatory.

3. _____ You can take any classes you want at college.

4. _____ The college amenities are only available to full-time, four-year students, and not to international program students.

5. _____ It's a good idea to get advice from an advisor when choosing your classes.

6. _____ All local stores and restaurants offer discounts if you show your student ID.

7. _____ The "Freshman 15" refers to the number of credit hours a freshman typically takes.

8. _____ Interjections should not be used in academic writing.

9. _____ You must be an Arts student to take painting or dance classes.

10. _____ If someone says, "Oops!" there could be a problem.

BY THE WAY . . .

The first year of college is usually known as *freshman year*. Students are called *freshmen*, or more commonly, *first-year students*. Second year is *sophomore* year; third is *junior* year; and the fourth and LAST year (yes, you made it . . . finally!) is called *senior* year. Everyone wants to be a senior!

Okay, did we say the *last* year? Yes, senior year is usually the last for a bachelor's degree, but students who continue for advanced degrees are simply *graduate* students. See Part 4 for more information about different degrees.

VOCABULARY

- **adaptor:** the device that allows your appliances to work with an electrical system
- **amenity:** a convenience
- **auditorium:** a very large room for presentations or lectures
- **BBQ:** barbecue; an outside party with food cooked on a grill
- **boxed lunch:** meal in a box, often provided to groups. A typical boxed lunch contains a sandwich, a piece of fruit, and a small bag of chips or cookies.
- **brochure:** folded paper with information, often with pictures, about events or activities
- ① **brunch:** not BReakfast, not Lunch. . . BRUNCH! (You can eat breakfast OR lunch foods . . . or both, ha!)
- ① **bye-bye:** another way to say good-bye
- **campus:** the buildings and outside areas of a college
- ① **check into:** get information about; learn about

- **delicious:** really great tasting! yum!
- **discount:** a lower price
- **dorm:** the place where you sleep as a first-year student
- **elective:** class that is not required, but that you take because it interests you
- **enroll:** officially sign up for a program; join a class
- **ESL:** English as a Second Language
- **exhibit:** show or demonstration
- **fabulous:** fantastic!
- **faculty:** instructors in a school
- **fast food:** Come on, you know this! It's food that can be made, served, and taken out quickly.
- **flyer:** paper with information about events or activities
- **food truck:** large vehicle where people prepare and sell food; similar to "street food" sold by street vendors
- ⓘ **freebie!:** something you get that you don't have to pay for! We LOVE freebies!
- **freshman 15:** the 15 pounds lots of first-year college students gain. Eat salad!
- **gain:** increase or add (like pounds, after eating all that take-out and junk food!)
- **genius:** someone who's really, really, REALLY smart!
- ⓘ **get down to business:** begin to get serious about something
- ⓘ **get it:** understand
- ⓘ **goodies:** things to enjoy, often yummy foods. Yes, please!
- ⓘ **guy:** a (male) person; in the plural (*guys*) means *people, friends* (male and female)
- ⓘ **handy:** useful
- **ice cream social:** a party with ... ICE CREAM treats!
- **ID:** Identification; proof that you are YOU!
- **jet lag:** that feeling of being very tired after a long airplane flight, especially from a different time zone. ICK!
- **junk food:** Come on, you know this! It's all the food that you shouldn't eat (but you do!) . . . like cookies, candy and chips. YUM—we want some junk food right now!
- **just in case:** not expecting something to happen, but planning for it if it does!
- **maintain:** keep up; be sure that something is still within rules

- **mandatory:** required
- **mug:** a large cup, often with a design
- ⓘ **nap:** a short sleep, often in the afternoon. Hey, I could use one right now!
- **nutritious:** good for you! having substances that the body needs to be healthy
- ⓘ **of course:** a phrase that emphasizes that something is very clearly true
- ⓘ **order out:** call a restaurant to order food to eat at home
- **orientation:** a program of learning about a new place
- ⓘ **out of the way:** completed so you don't have to worry about doing it later
- **overwhelmed:** feeling very stressed and anxious; feeling that you'll never understand everything
- **required course:** course that all students in your program must take
- **residence hall:** the building where students live while they're in college; also called a dorm (dormitory)
- **resources:** support; information or programs that can be helpful
- **right:** correct
- ⓘ **see you later:** what friends say when they are leaving each other; a way to say good-bye
- **semester:** the length of time for completing a course
- **seminar:** class consisting of a teacher and a small group of students; also, a conference
- **sensible:** thoughtful; smart
- **show:** provide for someone to see
- ⓘ **sign up:** write your name to become part of a group or activity
- ⓘ **so long:** another way to say good-bye
- **special pricing:** offering lower prices for certain groups
- **stress ball:** soft ball that you can squeeze in your hands to relieve anxiety or . . . um . . . . STRESS!
- **support:** help
- ⓘ **take advantage of:** make the most of a situation; use something that's available
- ⓘ **take-out:** food that you order by phone or with an app, then pick up to eat at home
- ⓘ **tons:** a lot of
- **tuition:** the cost to study at a school
- **tutor:** a person (often another student) who can help in an academic subject

- **tutoring:** meetings with someone who can give you extra help in an academic area
- **tutu:** the really cute skirt (usually made of a material called *tulle*) that ballerinas wear
- **venue:** place where concerts, sports events, parties, and other events happen
- ⓘ **what the heck:** a fun expression of surprise
- **wonder:** think about; question in your mind
- ⓘ **yum:** "It's delicious!"

USE YOUR WORDS!

Complete the sentences with a new word from the sections above. Try to do it without looking at the vocabulary list. Hey, we'll even help you by giving you the first letter! (You're welcome.) Answers are on page 223.

1. The best part about having a student ID is the **d**_____ at the bookstore.

2. It will be a great concert! It's in a small **v**_____, so the sound will be perfect!

3. There is so much going on at orientation that you might feel **o**_____ sometimes.

4. Hey, our favorite restaurant is now serving **b**_____ on weekends! We can sleep late, then eat breakfast/lunch whenever we want.

5. The worst part of a long flight is the **j**_____ you feel for a few days after you arrive.

6. Make sure you don't miss any **m**_____ sessions during orientation!

7. You'll need a nice long **n**_____ after orientation. All those activities are tiring!

8. It's a good idea to keep all the **f**_____ you collect at orientation. You'll need them to remember all the cool things available to you.

9. It's been a while since I took a math class, so I'll definitely be using that free **t**_____ service!

10. Wow, with all these calculus classes you're taking, you'll be a math **g**_____!

Let's talk about . . . MONEY!

When you were a **little kid**, did you **pretend** that you owned a toy store? (Ha, *we* did! We also pretended that we owned a candy store, but that's another story!) Maybe you had the coolest toys and **gadgets** in your little-kid store . . . all the cool things you wished you could buy in real life. In *our* little-kid **imaginary** store, our friends could "buy" our cool stuff for . . . **FREE**! Haha, yeah, that's right—we let our friends have the cool (pretend!) stuff for free. We know what you're thinking ... and you're right—we didn't make much money on our little pretend business, because, well, everything was . . . FREE!

Anyway, we're sorry to report that you will not find many stores **giving away** cool stuff for free like we did in our little-kid store, so we're here to help you figure out the money **situation**. And the first thing to know is that you'll hear plenty of slang terms for money. When you graduate, do you hope to get a job that pays a very high salary? Then you'll be *making bank*. Your friends will be impressed that you're making *big bucks*. You'll even be able to **spend** some *Benjamins* (hundred-dollar bills) on the latest new phone. And with all that *moolah* from your fabulous job, it will be no problem to spend a few hundred *smackers* to buy dinner for your friends. After all, they may still be paying several *grand* (thousand dollars) for their tuition. Hey, since you have all that *dough*, invite us to dinner, too!

If you're like us, you don't **carry around** a lot of **cash**. Why have a **wad** of bills and a **pocketful** of change when you can use plastic? (Or, even better, just swipe a finger on your phone!) If you use a credit card, the **cashier** (or the card reader machine) will ask, "**debit or credit**?" If you choose *debit*, the

POS payment

money will be **transferred** immediately out of the bank account that you **set up**. For a debit **transaction**, you'll need to enter your **PIN** (the four-**digit** secret number that you set up). If you choose *credit*, the money will be **charged** to your credit card account. You don't have to enter your PIN for a credit **purchase**, and the money doesn't come out of your bank account right away. You have a whole **billing cycle** not to worry about paying. But ha—just wait until you get that bill! Be really careful about this. Make sure that you **budget** your money so that you'll have enough to pay that bill. You'll get a statement of all your credit card charges each month, with the total amount you owe. The **statement** will also have a **minimum amount** due. There are two ways to pay your bill: the smart way (if you can afford it!) and the expensive way. The smart way is to pay the entire bill. Yeah, we know— that's painful, ha! But hey, we didn't tell you to buy all that crazy stuff! The expensive way is to pay only the *minimum amount* due. That's a percentage of the total amount. Sure, it looks better to pay the smaller amount, but if you pay only the minimum, the bank will charge **interest** on the **balance** (the rest of the amount you owe). That means you will owe what you spent on all those crazy purchases, PLUS the interest the bank charges. *Aaaaackkkk!*

 This may sound hard to believe if you do your banking using an app on your phone, but some people still pay for things using **checks**. They write a check for the amount of the purchase, the store sends the check, or an image of it, to the bank (usually electronically), and the bank takes the money from the checking account. When we pay for something using actual money (ha) instead of a debit/credit card or **wireless pay** system, we say we're paying "cash." Bills and **coins** are cash.

In the U.S., bills come in these amounts: $1, $5, $10, $20, $50, and $100. (Haha, we like the $100 bill best, but we never have any of those.) There's actually a $2 bill too, but you probably won't ever see one. Are you wondering about those **handsome** guys with the funny **haircuts** on those bills? They're past presidents or important people in U.S. history. Okay, we'll tell you their names in our chart on the next page, but you should know this: Not many Americans know who's on every bill! (Well, just about everyone knows Washington and Lincoln, but the other guys? Sorry!) And are you wondering about the important *women* in American history? They're not on the money ... yet! *Why* aren't they on the money? Excellent question! So things are about to change. The year 2020 **marks** the first time women will appear on U.S. bills. And it will be a woman taking the place of Andrew Jackson on the $20 bill. This recognizes the 100th anniversary of women's **right** to vote. Yay! (But, hey . . . why couldn't we be on the ONE HUNDRED DOLLAR bill?)

THINK ABOUT IT

People say, "Money can't buy happiness." Hmm. But money *can* buy . . . a Lamborghini! Money *can* buy a fancy apartment in New York City. In your opinion, does being able to buy nice things mean a person will be happy? Do you think using money to help others would make a person happy? How important do you think money should be in someone's life? If you get a great job after graduation, and you start making big bucks, what will you do with the money?

BY THE WAY . . .

Lots of times students go to a restaurant together. When the bill comes, there's an easy way to share the cost! If each person gives the **server** a credit card, the server will **split** the cost among the credit cards. (And, just to keep things interesting, the *bill* is also called the *check*.) When you get the receipt for your share of the bill/check, don't forget to tip the server!

LANGUAGE SPOT: BILLS! PAPER MONEY! CHANGE!

Money! What's it all about? What do we say when we talk about the **denominations**? Who are these people on the bills? And why are they there? Take a look at our money chart. No tip required.

WHAT DO WE SAY?		WHO IS IT?	WHY?
$1	a dollar; a single; a buck	George Washington	1st president of the U.S.
$5	a five	Abraham Lincoln	16th president of the U.S.
$10	a ten	Alexander Hamilton	1st Secretary of the Treasury
$20	a twenty	Andrew Jackson (to change in 2020)	7th president of the U.S.
$50	a fifty	Ulysses S. Grant	18th president of the U.S.
$100	a hundred; a C-note; a Benjamin	Benjamin Franklin	one of the **Founding Fathers** – He helped establish the United States of America.

- There's no $1,000 bill that people use, but there is a nickname for one thousand dollars: a *grand*. Students may say, "I can't fly home for the holidays because the ticket costs two *grand*."

- The abbreviation K is often used for *thousand*. "Wow! My tuition will be $30K next year." (We write the dollar sign, but we don't say *dollars*; we just say *30K*.)

Have you noticed? U.S. bills are all the same size and color. Ha, be careful! Don't mistake that twenty-dollar bill for one dollar! And, hey, look at the coins below . . . What's with the 10-cent coin being smaller than the 5-cent coin?

Coins! Change!

WHAT DO WE SAY?		WHO IS IT?	WHY?
1¢	one cent; a penny	Abraham Lincoln	16th president of the U.S.
5¢	5 cents; a nickel	Thomas Jefferson	3rd president of the U.S.
10¢	10 cents; a dime	Franklin D. Roosevelt	32nd president of the U.S.
25¢	twenty-five cents; a quarter	George Washington	1st president of the U.S.
50¢	fifty-cent piece; a half-dollar	John F. Kennedy	35th president of the U.S.
$1.00	dollar coin	Sacagawea	Native American wilderness guide

TRY IT!

How much money do you have in your pocket? Can you match the money amount to the way we say it? Write the number next to the words. Answers are on page 223.

| $1.25 | $1.00 | $45 | $50 | 75¢ |
| 10¢ | 25¢ | $3.15 | $1.50 | 50¢ |

1. _____ a dollar twenty-five

2. _____ two twenties and a five

3. _____ a dime

4. _____ fifty bucks

5. _____ two dimes and a nickel

6. _____ a quarter

7. _____ two nickels

8. _____ three fifteen

9. _____ three quarters

10. _____ a buck and a half

11. _____ half a dollar

12. _____ a buck and a quarter

13. _____ one fifty

14. _____ a fifty

15. _____ a single

DIALOGUE: AUDIO TRACK 4

A Weekend Away!

HE: Hey, I just came from the Student Activities Office. They have student discount tickets for the baseball game in Baltimore! They're half-price! HALF-PRICE!

SHE: Baltimore? You mean the Baltimore Orioles? I LOVE the Baltimore Orioles! They're my favorite baseball team! When is the game?

HE: This weekend. It's a night game on Saturday. Hey, maybe we can get a group of our orientation friends to go.

SHE: Wow, that would be fun! Is Baltimore far from campus? How would we get there?

HE: I already **looked into** that. We can take a bus—it's about a two-hour drive from here.

SHE: Hmm . . . I have a great idea. Let's get a group to share the cost . . . and maybe we can spend the weekend. I'd love to visit the Aquarium at the **Inner Harbor**.

HE: Hey, that's a great idea! We can **explore** Baltimore during the day, then go to the stadium for the game Saturday night. Camden Yards is a beautiful **stadium**, and it's right near the harbor.

SHE: Uh-oh.

HE: That doesn't sound good . . .

SHE: It's *not* good! I'm **broke**! I don't even have five bucks in my pocket!

HE: Ouch! Well, can you use your credit card?

SHE: Hmm. I'm not sure that's a good idea. I charged a lot of purchases last month when I shopped for things I needed for my dorm room. I checked my credit card bill online today . . . there's a really big balance, and the payment is due next week. Bye-bye, baseball tickets.

HE: Oh no, that's too bad. But do you know that you don't have to pay the total balance right away? You could just make the **minimum payment** this time, then **put money aside** next month to **pay off** the rest.

SHE: I'm not sure how that works . . . What's the "minimum payment"?

HE: Take a look at the bill online. There's a "**current** balance." That's the total amount that you owe, right up to today. Then there's a "statement balance." That shows the amount you owed when the billing period ended.

SHE: Yes! Yes! The statement balance *is* less than the current balance. So which one do I have to pay?

HE: Well, did you see a "minimum payment"?

SHE: Yeah. . . and that's just a small amount.

HE: That's the one you're *required* to pay.

SHE: PERFECT! I'll only pay the minimum payment this month; then I can afford to go to Baltimore! And I'll **pinch pennies** next month so I can pay the entire balance next time.

HE: Haha, that's the credit card trap! Be careful. Remember that the bank will add interest if you don't pay the full statement balance.

SHE: Oh boy—statement balance, current balance, minimum payment, interest, *aaaackkk!* . . . But it's the Baltimore Orioles! I HAVE to go! And after all—isn't that what credit cards are for—to pay for important things that you need when you don't have the cash? And I NEED to go to Baltimore! Let's GO, Orioles!

YOUR TURN!

How much do you remember from the previous sections? Write *True* or *False*. Answers on page 224.

1. _____ A store cashier is the person who collects payment for what you buy.

2. _____ If you say "credit" when you make your purchase, the money is immediately taken from your bank account.

3. _____ A credit card's online *statement balance* and *current balance* must always be the same.

4. _____ *Making bank* is a way to say you have a new job at a bank.

5. _____ A (small) dime is **worth** more than a (larger) nickel.

6. _____ Friends must pay cash if they want to share the cost in a restaurant.

7. _____ Your college may have tickets for students to attend off-campus events.

8. _____ Paper money in the U.S. is all the same size.

9. _____ Every American bill has the picture of an American president.

10. _____ If you're *broke*, you aren't feeling well.

BY THE WAY . . .

Don't be surprised if you never see a half-dollar or a dollar coin. Nobody uses them! Maybe it's because they're close in size to quarters. Or maybe people just don't want another coin **clinking** around in their pockets! You'll probably only get dollar coins as change from **vending machines** or at **laundromats**.

VOCABULARY

- **balance:** the remaining part of something, usually money owed
- **billing cycle:** the time (usually a month) between dates when you must pay a credit card bill
- ⓘ **broke:** having no money to spend
- **budget:** plan your spending carefully to be sure you have enough money
- ⓘ **carry around:** keep with you all the time
- **cash:** actual money!
- **cashier:** the person who takes the money for a purchase
- **charge:** the cost of something; also the way to pay later for something you buy now
- **check:** the paper form that is payment from a bank checking account; also, another word for the bill after a restaurant meal.
- **clink:** make a metal sound
- **coin:** metal money
- **credit:** a money account where purchases are paid monthly
- **current:** most recent; up-to-date
- **debit:** the amount taken out of a money account
- **denominations:** the value of money as shown on the bill or coin
- **digit:** the individual units in a number (0 – 9)
- **explore:** learn about by visiting many places
- **Founding Fathers:** the important men in American history who formed the new country: the United States of America
- **free:** you don't pay anything! Yay, we love free!
- ⓘ **gadgets:** small useful items or tools
- ⓘ **give away:** give something to someone for free
- **haircut:** the style of your hair; also, the cut to make your hair shorter
- **handsome:** good-looking!
- **harbor:** a calm place along the water where boats can stay
- **imaginary:** not real; something from your mind
- **Inner Harbor:** a tourist area around the harbor in Baltimore, Maryland. Go! Visit!
- **interest:** the amount a bank adds to money that you owe. Thanks, banks!
- **laundromat:** the place with washers and dryers where you go to clean your clothes
- ⓘ **little kid:** young child

- ⓘ **look into:** get information about something; investigate
- **mark:** make note of something; signify the importance of something
- **minimum amount:** lowest amount
- **minimum payment:** the lowest amount that you must pay
- **pay off:** pay the entire amount of a bill so that you owe nothing
- **PIN:** Personal Identification Number; the numbers that you choose as a security check for an account
- ⓘ **pinch pennies:** try not to spend money; be very careful about trying to save money
- **pocketful:** a lot of stuff in your pocket!
- **pretend:** act or dress as something you are not; act as if a situation is true
- **purchase:** buy; something that you pay for (yes—it's a verb AND a noun!)
- ⓘ **put money aside:** save
- **right:** correct; also, a privilege granted by law
- **server:** also called a waiter or waitress; the person who brings your food in a restaurant
- ⓘ **set up:** begin; establish
- **situation:** a problem; the facts or circumstances of an event
- **spend (money):** pay money to get something
- **spend (time):** use; pass
- **split:** divide, separate into parts; share
- **stadium:** the place where a sports event takes place
- **statement:** a listing of all purchases and payments on an account
- **transaction:** completion of some banking business
- **transfer:** move from one place to another
- **vending machine:** large machine with SNACKS. It takes coins or bills as payment.
- ⓘ **wad:** a big stack of bills (we would love to have a wad of cash!)
- **wireless pay:** the system of holding your phone near a device to pay for a purchase. Cool!
- **worth:** of value

USE YOUR WORDS!

Complete the sentences with new words from the section above. Choose from the words below. Answers are on page 224.

put aside	change	transfer	PIN	digit
statement	interest	wireless pay	purchase	vending machine

1. The advantage of a credit card is that you can _____ something you need, even if you don't have enough cash at the time.

2. I hope there's a _____ nearby. I want a snack, but I don't have time to go to the dining hall.

3. I just checked my account . . . I think I need to _____ some money into my school account.

4. You'll need to enter your _____ if you pay by debit card. Keep the number private!

5. Wow, that was an expensive can of Coke! I put a five in the vending machine, but it didn't give me _____ .

6. I'm excited about the vacation! I've already started to _____ some money so I'll have plenty to spend when I get there.

7. If you don't pay the entire credit card bill, you'll be charged _____ on the unpaid amount.

8. Your bank can send you a paper _____ if you prefer, but most people like to check it online.

9. Each unit (0 – 9) in a number is called a _____.

10. I love using the _____ system at my neighborhood supermarket. I just hold my phone near the device at the cashier, and poof! I've paid!

FUN WITH IDIOMATIC EXPRESSIONS: Speaking of Money . . .

- **a dime a dozen:** very common; not special
  *Food trucks are **a dime a dozen** on big college campuses. No one needs the cafeteria!*

- **add one's two cents:** give your opinion about something
  *I'm going to that meeting about the new rule so I can **add my two cents** before they make a decision.*

- **cash a check:** Do people still get paper checks?! It's a small paper form (our favorite is from our job, and it's called a PAYCHECK) that says how much money the bank will give you. Banks will give you cash when you sign the check.
  *My bank isn't nearby . . . I wonder if I can **cash this check** at the ATM.*

- **cost a pretty penny:** be very expensive
  *Yeah, the latest tablet computer is cool, but it **costs a pretty penny.***

- **look (or feel) like a million bucks/dollars:** look or feel FABULOUS
  *After wearing jeans all week, he **felt like a million bucks** in a jacket and tie.*

- **making big bucks:** having a job that pays a lot of money
  *Now that you have that fancy college degree, you can start **making big bucks!***

- **pinch pennies:** be very, very careful about spending money; try to save money
  *Hey! Are you eating pizza every day because you're **pinching pennies**, or because you really, really like pizza?*

- **short of money/cash:** broke; strapped for cash; not having much money
  *Yes! I'm going on the trip to Baltimore! I missed the last trip because I was **short of cash** until I got the job at the library.*

- **strapped for cash:** not having a lot of money; broke
  *I can't go to out to dinner with you this week. I'm a little **strapped for cash** until I get my paycheck.*

- **turn on a dime:** make a very sudden turn, like the fancy car I wish I had!
  *He's an expert cyclist—he can make that bike **turn on a dime**.*

 TRY IT!

What expression from the list above works best in these sentences? Answers are on page 225.

1. Wow, a Maserati! I guess Keith is _____ in his new job. Those fancy cars (2.) _____.

3. Sam is a really smart guy who reads everything. He also has an opinion about everything, so he _____ at every meeting.

4. Don't worry about getting funny pictures in Times Square. Those crazy characters are _____.

5. I just bought all the textbooks for my classes, so I'm a little _____ right now. No fancy dinners this week!

 JUST FOR FUN!

Yes! For YOU! Are you ready? Okay, only for YOU—Here are some. . .

BIG BUCKS:

Wait . . . Do you mean these are not the big bucks you were hoping for? HAHA! But they *are* bucks . . . just not the ones that will buy you a Lamborghini! These bucks are male deer. (And the plural form of *deer* is . . . yes, *deer!*) You can tell male deer by the **antlers** on their heads. A female deer is called a *doe*. Haha, not *dough*, like another slang word for money. And just in case you were wondering . . . a baby deer is called a *fawn*. And now, ahem, *dear* students, let's move on. . .

TIP: What's in a Name?

Americans very often have three names: first, middle, last. The last name is the family name. The first and middle names are ones that are special to the parents—because they just like the names, or because the names honor someone special. Most Americans just use their first and last names, and sometimes the middle initial; but in some parts of the country it's not unusual for people to be called by their middle names. And just to keep it tricky . . . sometimes the middle name is a last name (from the other **spouse**, for example)! Take a look:

- Our friend *Charlotte Brynn Murphy* is called *Charlotte* by her friends. When she signs important papers, she uses her middle initial, and she signs *Charlotte B. Murphy*.

- In Charleston, South Carolina, *Lynn Marshall Turner*'s friends and family call him *Marshall*. He signs his papers *L. Marshall Turner*, using only his first initial.

While we're talking about names . . . Last names can get a little **complicated**. In the past, when a couple married, one person would change to the spouse's family name. When a woman married, she would change her **maiden name** to her spouse's last name. Now when they marry, many people choose to keep their own family names, and not change names at all. Sometimes both people will take both names. So when they marry, Chris *Smith* and Jamie *Taylor* may become Chris *Smith-Taylor* and Jamie *Smith-Taylor*. Wow! But if they have a child (named Jesse *Smith-Taylor*) who marries Devin *Jones-Davis* ... [you see where this is going, don't you?] . . . does that person become Jesse *Smith-Taylor-Jones-Davis*? OH NO! My head hurts!

 TIP: At the Stadium

Are you going to the Baltimore Orioles game? Or to any baseball game? Or to any sports event at all? Before sports events begin in the U.S., it's **customary** to sing the national anthem ("The Star-Spangled Banner"). Performers consider it an honor to lead the singing. During the anthem everyone in the stadium stands and faces the flag. Men should remove their hats. Of course, visitors from other countries are not expected to sing the anthem, but it's important to stand and be respectful and **attentive**.

Do you know any of these people who are famous for their singing of "The Star-Spangled Banner"? Google them! Listen! WOW!

- Josh Groban, with Flea (of the band Red Hot Chili Peppers)
- Beyoncé
- Whitney Houston
- Kelly Clarkson

Okay, this "Star-Spangled Banner" wasn't at a sports event, but it's **considered** a **classic** of rock 'n roll: Jimi Hendrix playing at Woodstock. At WOODSTOCK, folks! And if you don't know what Woodstock was, stop reading right now! Go look it up immediately! Woodstock is a huge part of American cultural history. WOODSTOCK, baby!

ROAD TRIP: Washington, D.C.

Baseball game in Baltimore? Let's head a little south (it's only about an hour) to Washington, D.C. Sure, you've seen *pictures* of the nation's capital . . . how about an actual visit to put *yourself* into the picture? D.C. is a city full of parks, green spaces, and fountains. Walk the National Mall from the Capitol (it's the building where the U.S. Congress meets) to the Potomac River. It's a beautiful green space with monuments and museums all along the way. There are memorials to presidents and to those who have served the country in war. The Smithsonian is a collection of museums: 19 of them! And (with only an exception or two) they are all *free*! You can even get a plan for your visit. Go to the website *www.si.edu* for really cool information on how to get from place to place easily.

And don't forget that you can actually tour inside many of the important government buildings. Just about all of the U.S. government buildings, memorials, and museums have information in many languages. If you don't see a brochure in your language, just ask. (And did we mention, most of the museums are FREE! Yay!)

Cool D.C. tip: It may be possible to take a tour of the **White House**. Non-U.S. citizens must **arrange** this through their countries' embassies. At the website *embassy.org* you can find out how to contact your embassy. And hey, take a look at the website *Washington.org* too. Enter "international visitor" into the search box, and you'll find enough cool things to do to keep you busy for a month! Have fun! Say hello to the President for us!

☑ QUICK FACTS

☑ What's the largest state? Don't Google it—take a look at a map! Did you guess Texas? Close, but . . . WRONG! Look again. It's Alaska!

☑ The U.S. is one (very big!) country, with many parts. There are 50 states. Each state has its own capital city, and each state has its own laws. For example, the **speed limit** on highways is decided by the states. Some laws (the legal age for voting, for example) are decided by the federal government, and they apply to all the states.

ANY QUESTIONS?

Is it *the U.S.*? Is it *USA*? Is it *America*? Is it the *United States*? YES! It is all of the above! Does it matter which one you use? Not really. It's all the same place! In very formal usage (presidential speeches, for example) the country may be called "The United States of America." When people are being patriotic they may say things like, "We love America!" But usually when talking about the country, Americans will simply say "the U.S." Here's an example: "If you go anywhere in the U.S., you will probably be able to find a fast food restaurant!"

VOCABULARY

- **antlers:** horns on some (usually male) animals
- **arrange:** plan
- **attentive:** showing care; thoughtful
- **classic:** something that, throughout time, most people agree is excellent
- **complicated:** tricky; having many things to think about
- **considered:** believed to be; thought
- **customary:** usual
- **maiden name:** a woman's last name before she marries
- **speed limit:** the fastest you're allowed to go. Leave the Lamborghini home!
- **spouse:** the person someone is married to
- **The White House:** You've seen it! It's the big (white!) building where the president lives and works.

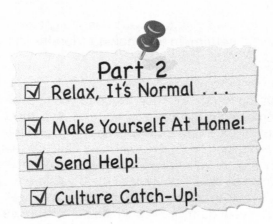

Part 2

- ☑ Relax, It's Normal . . .
- ☑ Make Yourself At Home!
- ☑ Send Help!
- ☑ Culture Catch-Up!

RELAX, IT'S NORMAL (CULTURE SHOCK)

Are you **exhausted**? Are you wondering if orientation activities are actually some kind of crazy test that **only the strong survive**?! HA! No, believe it or not, all those **contests** and campus tours and **talks** and games are really to help you start feeling comfortable in your new home. Yes, the campus is now your NEW HOME for the next four years! Hmm, does it **feel like home**? Or does it sometimes feel like you've landed on an **alien** planet with strange foods and strange customs? Relax! That's **normal**! And it's possible that being so exhausted after being so busy with new things is making you think of your *real* home . . . so far away. And your family . . . *so far away.* And your friends . . . *so far away.* With everything that you know and love so far away, you may start feeling a little **culture shock**. Relax! It's normal! Culture shock is the **stress** lots of people feel in a new and very different place. It's feeling uncomfortable with the way people do things. It's feeling like an **outsider** . . . that you don't **fit in**. It may be feeling that you've lost the **confidence** in yourself that got you here in the first place. And it may even be . . . (this is a big one) . . . **missing** your FABULOUS home food and trying to figure out what crazy things these crazy American people are eating! RELAX! It's normal!

Everyone gets **homesick** sometimes. And it's helpful to know that culture shock is . . . normal! The **good news** is that the feeling of "What the heck am I doing here?!" will start to go away as you get more and more comfortable, and start **settling in** and **making friends**. And we're here to help you figure out HOW to do that! Yay!

Chances are you met lots of new people at orientation. GREAT! That's a **head start** on making friends. But now it's up to you to **take the initiative**. As you see kids on campus that you saw at orientation, try not to be **shy**— say hi! Think about this: If you're too shy to say hello, and the other person is too shy to say hello, then NOBODY WILL SAY HELLO! That's *not* a good way to make friends! If you're in an elevator with someone, you could say, "Wow, this elevator is so slow." Or in line at the bookstore you could say, "I'm glad the line is moving quickly." If you're in the dining hall, and you see a **couple of** kids from your dorm, you could say something like, "Hi. Can I join you?" or, "Hi. We were on the same team at orientation. **Mind** if I join you?" They'll say, "Sure! **Have a seat**." In class you could say, "Oh, hi. We were both at the meeting the other night. Hey, is that seat **taken**?" or "Hi. Aren't you in the Williams dorm?"

Be a **joiner**! You'll probably see signs **all over** campus about activities and clubs and **social events**. GO! Try everything!  Multi-cultural events are a great way to find people who share your background and who are interested in learning about other cultures. Artistic events can **showcase** student design, dance, theater, and art. Campus **clubs** and organizations are **open** to anyone who's interested; you don't have to just **stick with** your course of studies. Yes, even math majors are welcome to join the Art Club! (Haha, but we want to know why the heck *anyone* would be a MATH MAJOR! *aaaackkk! We're scared of the math monster!*) Of course, math majors will probably be interested in the Math Club too, but **feel free** to join any group that interests you. For example, if you plan to study business, you may be interested in the Young **Entrepreneurs** organization, or Women in Engineering. But does that mean you can't stick with your love of classical (or rock & roll!) music? OF COURSE NOT! Join a music club too! Join the orchestra! Go to concerts! Culture and the arts and FUN are important parts of student life on campus! There's an old expression in English: "All work and no play makes Jack a **dull** boy." And there's a newer expression, too: "Work hard, PLAY hard!"

Of course you're here to study, but remember this: Colleges and universities WANT students to participate in the life of the school! After all, active students are what make a college **vibrant** and exciting. Are you interested in **politics** and making changes in the way government does things? Join a political **action group**! No matter what your politics are, there will be others who share your ideas. Are you interested in **volunteering**, and doing things that help people in need? Join a social **activist** group! You'll meet people in the community who design programs to help others. Our favorite group helps people in cities make **community gardens**. The group finds **abandoned** city **lots** that may be filled with trash, and the students clean them up. They contact community leaders for permission, and before you know it, the trash-filled space becomes an **urban** garden where people in the community can learn to care for (and enjoy) growing plants: tomatoes and peppers and peas, beets and beans, cabbage and corn . . . and flowers! Thanks to a student activist group, people in the city now have a beautiful garden, with **access** to fresh fruits and vegetables that they grow themselves.

Another way of making friends on most college campuses is participating in **Greek life**. Ha—do you think that means heading to the airport for another travel adventure? No! (But the idea of **jetting off** to a sunny Greek island sure sounds good to us!) *Greek life* means joining a **fraternity** (men) or **sorority** (women). Not too many, but some of these groups are **co-ed**. These are large, very strong social groups with different purposes: some with professional or **community service** interests, some with academic or leadership goals, and some with purely **social** goals. The groups are a good way for people to help each other develop professionally, and to analyze career possibilities. When someone becomes a member of a **frat** or a sorority, they are connected to other members of the group anywhere. Some people think this is good for professional **networking**, because members of the group in business and the community often like to support their "brothers" or "sisters." The connection among members is very strong, and lasts even past college. Once you're accepted into the group, you're considered a fraternity brother or sorority sister for life.

Fraternities and sororities often do many projects to help people in the community. They plan fun activities to **raise money** for local hospitals and children's groups. But they are also very proud of how they **stick together**. They often have "**houses**"

on college campuses (and off-campus) across the country, where members of the group can live while they're at school. And of course these houses are used for hanging out . . . and, um . . . fun social events too.

However you decide to make friends and have fun at college, there's something for everyone! Get involved! Do something you love! HAVE FUN!

THINK ABOUT IT

Sure, we know you miss home. And we know you really miss the familiar foods that you love, ha! But remember this: Everyone in your program is probably feeling exactly the same way, so you already have something **in common** with other students! But even more important—you have a **sense of adventure** . . . or you wouldn't be here! Your excitement about having new experiences is another thing that you share with your **classmates**! How can you use your interest in new things and new places to develop new friendships? Go on— have confidence in yourself, and have an adventure!

BY THE WAY . . .

Not everyone thinks that joining a fraternity or sorority is a good way to meet people. Many of these organizations require students to apply to become members, and they won't accept everyone. And, although colleges **strictly forbid** it, some groups practice *hazing*—a process of making new members do difficult or dangerous things. Some fraternity or sorority houses are off-campus, and there are sometimes reports of loud parties, and dangerous or disrespectful behavior toward the neighbors. If joining a very **close-knit** group like a fraternity sounds good to you, be sure to learn about the group's interests and **reputation** first!

LANGUAGE SPOT: ACADEMIC WORDS—GREEK AND LATIN

Many of the words that we use in English come from Greek and Latin. *Fraternity* comes from the Latin word *frater*, which means brother. *Sorority* comes from *soror*—sister. Okay, so the *Greek* fraternity/sorority system words come from *Latin*, fraternity names are usually three *Greek* letters, and the whole system began at *American* colleges. Haha, don't try to figure it out! But while we're talking about Latin and Greek, let's take a look at some common academic language. Here are some words that you will see in some form (and that you should use!) in academic writing. Um, do we need to mention that they are (or come from) . . . Greek and Latin?

GREEK

- **aristocracy:** high social class in some societies
  *His **aristocratic** family was very rich and important, so he was treated like a prince.*

- **chronos:** time
  *Our history professor explained the **chronological** order of events leading to the war.*

- **chronic:** happening again and again, time after time after time . . . as an illness that doesn't go away
  *She always has candy mints for her **chronic** cough. (But we think she just likes mints, ha.)*

- **dogma:** system of beliefs accepted without question as true
  *The professor expressed her opinion as if it were **dogma**.*

- **ethos:** the spirit or moral character of a person (or culture)
  *She was **ethical** in everything she did, so people trusted her.*

- **genesis:** the beginning of something
  *The author discussed the **genesis** of his idea for the book.*

- **hierarchy:** the levels in an organization
  *He spent the first day at work learning about the **hierarchy** of the company: workers – managers – vice-presidents – president.*

- **paradox:** something that seems to be impossible or opposite, but is true.
  *She's a **paradox**—she loves going out with a large group of friends, but she hates crowds.*

- **phobia:** an extreme fear of something
  *Her worst **phobia** is a fear of the ocean. No beach vacation for her!*

- **plethora:** more of something than you need
  *He used a **plethora** of examples to support his argument.*

LATIN

- **alma mater:** the school someone attended
  *She went on to a successful career in government, and she was always grateful to her **alma mater** for her excellent education.*

- **circa:** approximately
  *The baseball stadium was built **circa** 1950.*

- **impromptu:** without preparation or planning
  *The best part of today's history class was the **impromptu** debate among the students.*

- **per annum:** every year
  *With her new college degree she was making more money **per annum** than her friends.*

- **per capita:** for each person
  *In Economics 101 we learned which countries have the highest **per capita** income.*

- **re:** in reference to; about
  *The professor's email said, "**Re** our meeting—Let's change the time to 2:30."*

- **sic:** exactly as it is (used to show that a mistake is as the original writer wrote it)
  *The newspaper printed an interesting article about stoodents [**sic**].*

- **status quo:** the situation as it is now
  *Some students wanted to change the school's grading policy, but the university kept the **status quo**.*

- **verbatim:** using exactly the same words
  *To explain how the politician's ideas supported her beliefs, she quoted his speech **verbatim**.*

- **vice versa:** the other way around
  *The students had great respect for their teachers, and **vice versa**.*

TRY IT!

Choose one of the Greek or Latin words from the previous pages to complete the sentences. Answers are on page 225.

1. It's hard to choose from the _____ of activities available!

2. To have a great friendship you need to respect your friend, and _____.

3. It's important to understand the _____ within the university so you know who has the answers to questions that you may have.

4. It seems like a _____, but having a good social life can help with your academic life.

5. Have fun at college! In later years you'll have great memories of your _____.

6. One orientation activity was to have new students line up in _____ order of their birthdays.

7. She couldn't go to class when she was sick, so I told her _____the professor's instructions for the assignment.

8. On the last day of class, the students and the professors gathered for an _____ party. FUN!

9. Her sociology project analyzed how the _____ of the community determined which leaders it elected.

10. When the professor explained the _____ of the political movement, the students understood why so many people in the community became involved.

DIALOGUE: AUDIO TRACK 5

First Day of Classes

HE: Hi. Wow, this class is crowded. Is the seat next to you taken?

SHE: Nope, it's all yours.

HE: Thanks. Hey, I think I know you. Didn't you sign up for the video production club at orientation?

SHE: Yes! That explains it—I *thought* you looked familiar! Ha, but I have to say—after all those orientation activities, EVERYONE on this campus looks familiar! It's nice to see you again.

HE: Nice to see you too. I know what you mean about orientation . . . It was great getting to meet so many people, but I thought my head would explode trying to remember everything the staff was talking about! That's why I signed up **on the spot**—I was afraid when I got home I'd never remember where to find the video club!

SHE: HA—that is *exactly* what I was thinking! Sign up now before I lose the information! Where are you from?

HE: Cordoba. It's a city in the south of Spain. How about you?

SHE: Well, I was born in New Jersey, but my family moved around a lot. My dad's in the military, so we've lived all over the world. I've lived in Japan, South Korea, Germany . . . and we've been in England for the past several years. My high school alma mater is in London.

HE: Wow, that's pretty cool!

SHE: Yeah, it was kind of hard moving so much when I was a kid, but now I really appreciate all the cultures I've been able to experience. I've shared my culture with some great international friends, and vice versa. I've never been to Spain, though. Do you miss it?

HE: Oh wow, yes! Cordoba's a beautiful city, but what I really miss is the food.

SHE: Ha, I know what you mean! Family, friends . . . and FOOD!

HE: I think that's the hardest thing for me to get used to here in the U.S. Our meals in Spain are so different—most of the time everyone relaxes at meals. We **take our time**. Here everything seems so . . . I don't know . . . fast. I miss sharing big dishes of fresh vegetables, and fish, and olives, and rice . . . and . . . Oh, man, STOP ME!

SHE: I know what you mean. Starbucks is great, but I haven't had a really good cup of tea since I arrived.

HE: Oh boy, now you have me thinking about home! I guess I'm feeling a little homesick. My sister and I are really **close** . . . But we **chat** just about every day, so it's not too bad. We text, Skype, email . . . all the social networking platforms. I guess I have just about every video messaging app on my phone! Anyway, I've been so busy getting settled in here that I haven't had too much time to think about missing home.

SHE: Right. And don't forget that the first video production meeting is next week. I'm really **looking forward to** that. Are you going?

HE: Yeah, I'm planning to go. Hmm. But now that you mention it . . . I don't think I remember where we're supposed to meet. Do you?

SHE: Yeah. The studio's in Russell Hall, across campus. It's right near the dining hall . . . about a ten-minute walk from here. I'm heading that way right after class if you want me to show you where it is.

HE: Oh, great. No, I know where Russell Hall is. Hey, my next class isn't until 3:00, so if you're heading that way, maybe we can **grab** lunch.

SHE: Sure—I'm always hungry! And this is my last class of the day, so **I'm definitely in** for lunch. Hey, we can make it an impromptu "getting to know you" party!

HE: Sounds good. But did you say this is your *last* class of the day? Wow—nice!

SHE: Well, yes . . . and no. My first class was at 8 this morning. That is definitely *not* nice. I'm kind of a **night owl** and getting to that early class on time was really tough. Man, I hope it gets easier.

HE: Well, as my grandmother used to say, "**The early bird catches the worm.**"

SHE: HA! No thanks—I'll **pass** on the worm. I'd rather **sleep in** and grab a nice American breakfast sandwich on the way to a later class. No worms included.

HE: Well, worm or no worm, I think your last class of the day is about to start. Here comes the professor.

YOUR TURN!

What do you remember from the previous sections? Write *True* or *False* for each statement. Answers are on page 225.

1. _____ It's normal for students to feel homesick when they're far from home.

2. _____ International students who have researched their new country won't experience culture shock.

3. _____ Culture shock will never go away because customs are so different.

4. _____ It's considered polite to wait for the other student to speak to you first in a conversation.

5. _____ You should join clubs related to your major field of study.

6. _____ Men and women can join fraternities.

7. _____ Most students prefer to participate in "Greek life" to establish friendships.

8. _____ The biggest problem when making new friends is that students from very different cultures have nothing in common.

9. _____ If there isn't a club that interests you at the university, you should find an activity in the community instead.

10. _____ If you like gardens and planting, you should not choose a city college.

BY THE WAY . . .

Every college and university has a Student Activities Office. You should definitely **check out** all the information available there. Art, music, dance, business, sports, social causes, environmental groups, religious groups, fun activities, travel adventures—there are campus organizations to interest just about every student, and the Student Activities Office will help you find one that's perfect for you. And hey, if you prefer, you can organize your own fun group. (Hmm. In fact, we've always wanted to join a "**Peanut Butter** and **Jelly** Club"! Sign us up for the **PB&J** club!)

VOCABULARY

- **abandoned:** left alone
- **access:** get
- **action group:** a group of people who make plans and do things to improve something
- **activist:** a person who actively does things to support an issue or change
- **alien:** an extraterrestrial creature; a creature from outer space; also, something strange
- **all over:** everywhere
- ⓘ **chances are:** it is likely; it's probable
- ⓘ **chat:** talk informally
- ⓘ **check out:** research; learn about
- **classmate:** a person you go to school with
- **close-knit:** very connected; having a very strong feeling of togetherness
- **close:** connected
- **club:** a group of people who share an interest in an activity or a subject
- **co-ed:** for males and females
- **community garden:** a place where people in the neighborhood can enjoy growing plants
- **community service:** doing good work to help the local people
- **confidence:** believing that you, or someone else, can do something
- **contest:** competition
- ⓘ **couple of:** two or three
- **culture shock:** when everything seems strange and you feel uncomfortable
- **definitely:** for sure! no question!
- **dull:** boring
- ⓘ **early bird catches the worm:** a saying (proverb) that means someone who starts doing things early will be successful
- **entrepreneur:** a person who starts a new business from a creative idea
- **exhausted:** very, very, VERY tired. Take a nap!
- **feel:** seem
- ⓘ **feel free:** be comfortable doing something you want to do
- ⓘ **feel like:** want to
- ⓘ **feel like home:** feel that you belong; feel that you know the place or situation very well

- ⓘ **fit in:** seem like part of a group; be accepted as part of a group
- ⓘ **frat:** fraternity
- • **fraternity:** a type of social club, usually for male students
- ⓘ **good news:** the advantageous part of a situation that may have a down side
- ⓘ **grab:** get
- • **Greek life:** fraternities and sororities
- ⓘ **have a seat:** Please sit down.
- • **hazing:** a (secret) process of making new members of a club do difficult or dangerous things—this is an activity that is NOT allowed
- ⓘ **head start:** begin before others
- • **homesick:** feeling sad when you are away from home; missing the people, places, and food of home
- • **house:** the building where fraternities or sororities meet socially, or live
- ⓘ **I'm in:** I want to be included! I want to do this too!
- • **in common:** the same; sharing something
- ⓘ **it's all yours:** you can have it!
- • **jelly:** a sweet spread made from fruit (no seeds). Grape jelly is the best for a PB&J!
- ⓘ **jet off:** fly away someplace
- ⓘ **joiner:** someone who likes to take part in things
- ⓘ **look forward to:** be really excited about something about to happen soon
- • **lot:** section of land
- • **make friends:** get to know, and have fun with, new people
- ⓘ **mind:** "Do you mind?" "Is it okay?"
- • **miss:** feel sad thinking about people or things far away
- • **network:** meet other people with your interests, often for business purposes
- ⓘ **night owl:** someone who likes to stay up late
- ⓘ **nope:** no
- • **normal:** ordinary
- ⓘ **on the spot:** right there and then; immediately
- ⓘ **only the strong survive:** usually said in a funny way: you have to be strong to overcome a difficult situation
- • **open:** available

- **outsider:** a person who does not belong to a group
- ⓘ **pass:** decide not to do something
- ⓘ **PB&J:** peanut butter and jelly sandwich. YUM!
- **peanut butter:** ha, the best food in America! A spread made of crushed peanuts—it can be creamy, smooth or crunchy, with bits of peanuts
- **politics:** issues about the government and the people who are in government
- **raise money:** get money from people to support the good work of a group
- **reputation:** the opinion people have about a group or a person
- **sense of adventure:** wanting to do unusual or difficult things
- ⓘ **settle in:** feel comfortable in a new place
- **showcase:** display; show so others can see
- **shy:** quiet; not comfortable starting conversations
- ⓘ **sleep in:** YAY! Stay in bed for an extra long time
- **social event:** informal gathering of people, e.g., at a party
- **social:** friendly
- **sorority:** a type of social club, usually for female students
- ⓘ **sounds good:** I like the idea of that; I agree
- ⓘ **stick together:** support each other as a group
- ⓘ **stick with:** don't get bored by; continue doing something even after a long time
- **stress:** worry
- **strictly forbid:** very, *very* strongly refuse to allow some activity or behavior
- **take the initiative:** lead an action; start doing something instead of waiting for someone else to start
- ⓘ **take your time:** Slow down! There's no need to do this quickly.
- **taken** (a seat): someone else has planned to sit in that seat
- **talk:** an explanation of a topic, service, or situation
- **urban:** about a city or town (It's from the LATIN word for city: *urbs*!)
- **vibrant:** lively; exciting and interesting; colorful
- **volunteer:** give your free time to do something to help others
- **worm:** ICK!! It's that long little creature with no legs that lives in dirt. Birds think they're delicious! (We're glad we're not birds!)

USE YOUR WORDS!

Here are some phrases from this section. Put the best phrase into each sentence in the paragraph below. You may need to change the form of the verb. Answers are on page 226.

check out   sign up for   stick with
feel like home   sleep in   take the initiative
fit in   stick together   take your time
look forward to

It may seem very different when you first start college, but don't worry! You'll soon feel that you (1) _____ just fine! A great way to make friends is to (2) _____ an activity or club, but it's always best to (3) _____ what is involved first. It should be something fun, that you (4) _____ each week. Haha, but here's some advice: If you like to (5) _____ like us, DO NOT choose a 6 A.M. running club! It should be an activity or club that won't get boring after a short time. Choose something that you will (6) _____ and want to continue doing. A lot of activities sound like fun, but don't make a decision too quickly. (7) _____ and choose the perfect thing for you. You'll have fun, and you and the people you meet may become a great group of friends who really (8) _____ and support each other. It won't take long before your new college really starts to (9) _____. Ha . . . well, *home* without your cool home food! New friends and new fun— aren't you happy that you (10) _____ and joined that club?

MAKE YOURSELF AT HOME!

Here you are, thousands of miles from home . . . Hmm, or maybe not! By now you've **certainly** seen how many English language learners there are on campus. You've probably met many of them. But lots of students who are studying English AND regular college courses have lived in the U.S. for many years. Maybe they've thought about taking classes close to home, at this college, right in their neighborhood, and they've finally decided to just *go ahead and do it!* Maybe they've decided to complete an education they started many years ago. Maybe they want to study a new **field** to get a better job. And maybe they've decided that they just love to learn new stuff! (Hey—that's us! We love learning new things all the time. Hmm—except math. We don't ever love learning new math stuff, haha!)

Colleges welcome "**non-traditional**" students. These are usually adult learners, many of whom have jobs and families. Hey, maybe you're one of those people. Yay, you! Attending college is the perfect way to learn English AND learn skills to start on the path to a new **career**. If you are one of these people, let us just say this: We are amazed by your ability to **multi-task**! Wow, working **full-time** AND coming to school for evening or weekend classes! And **juggling** family responsibilities! Yes, WOW! (We're pretty sure we would fall asleep in class . . . and we DO NOT RECOMMEND that!)

Of course, many students coming back to college after a long time take only one or two courses. We know what you're thinking: "It's not so bad—we're just **part-time** students." HA! We think you're fabulous! We would be part-time CRAZY on a job-college-homework schedule, even with just one or two classes! And we can't even think about you students who work and take full **course loads**. We're exhausted just *thinking* about that! Of course, as a **commuter** student you can enjoy all the comforts of home . . . because you ARE home! When class is over you can just **crank up** the music in your car and drive back to your own **comfy** home. Hmm. Or maybe not . . . You may want to **stick around**! Most places have a plethora of activities for commuter students. It's very important for ALL students to feel like they're part of the **dynamic** college community. Everyone adds something special to the **student body,** and it's always more fun to share different experiences. Welcome, commuter students! Let's go grab a snack!

Commuter students may be lucky that they can go home to their nice comfy sofas, and grab snacks from their nice full **fridges,** but for many students **going away to school** is an important (and fun!) part of the college experience. Let the games begin!

Colleges and universities in the U.S. are always trying to **attract** the best students. How do they do this? Well, think about it: Why did *you* choose *this* college? Students want a school with an **exemplary** reputation. They want interesting courses in their field of study, and they want **outstanding** instructors. Some students choose a college because it's located near a city where they want to spend time. Well, a college can't change its location, and *all* colleges try to have the

best courses and faculty. So **how else** can a school make *you* want to choose it? HA! It's the great university competition! Who has the coolest campus? Who has the best student restaurants? (Ha, you know *we* would pick the one with the best FOOD!) Who has the best **fitness center**? And, of course, who has the best student **housing**?

There are tons of choices for living at school. There are traditional residence halls (also called *dormitories*) where you may share a room with another person (or two). At large universities these residence halls are often **high-rise** buildings. In the **dorm,** many rooms on a floor share one space for bathrooms and showers. Put on your **bathrobe** and **fluffy** bunny **slippers,** and bring your fancy soap and shampoo down the hall to the showers. Don't forget your towel!

Most colleges require first-year students to live in a residence hall on campus. You may be surprised to learn that there are a lot of **options** for these dorms. Lots of choices! You can choose a "quiet floor" where **blasting** music and making noise are forbidden. Maybe you want a residence hall that has a special space for your religious practice. Many American dorms are co-ed, so if you want a men-only or women-only building, be sure to say so when you request your room. Ask what choices are available.

When you choose your dorm, you'll also have a chance to think about **roommates**. Most universities have an online system that allows freshmen to find a roommate with similar interests. Do you love soccer? You may find another person who loves soccer to share your room. Do you like to study quietly in your room? You probably don't want a roommate who likes to blast music! You and your roommate will have a chance to communicate online before you even get to campus. Choose wisely! If you're a **party animal** and your roommate is a **bookworm**, things could get tricky!

Before you know it, it's **move-in day** at the dorms. Haha, we hope you didn't forget the aspirin, because by the end of the day, you will **ache** all over! Oops! Did we forget to tell you? You can't bring your piano, ha!

When the boxes are unpacked, the fun part begins—making this new "home" really feel like *home* to you. Residence halls have very strict rules about what is allowed, and the rules are strictly **enforced**. Be sure you know . . . and obey! . . . the rules.

Do you want to pack your **pooch**? ☒ No pets!

Do you picture purple and pink? ☒ No painting!

Do you love the taste of toast? ☒ **Toss** that toaster!

It's pretty simple: Anything that could be a safety hazard—or a fire hazard—**forbidden**! Anything that could be a health risk—forbidden. Anything that could damage the room—forbidden. And of course (do we even need to mention this?), anything that is illegal is **absolutely** forbidden. You can't have cooking devices in your room, but dorms have a kitchen available, sometimes one on every floor. Yes, this is a shared kitchen . . . ahem, and you may learn that not every student always obeys the clean-up-when-you're-finished rule. But we know *you* will!

Student safety is a **top priority** of university officials, and they will be very clear about **procedures** and **safety features** when you arrive on campus. In fact, we hate to be the ones to tell you this, but you will probably be **hopping** out of bed, and out of the building at 3 A.M. more times than you want to think about! We don't know why those fire alarms seem to **go off** at 3 A.M., but we do know that any time you hear it, you need to **evacuate** the building immediately. Officials will say when it's safe to return. Sorry to wake you from that sweet dream you were having . . .

The college will be very clear about what you *can't* have in your room, but the fun is in decorating with things you *can* have! Of course you'll have pictures of Pookie, your little pooch, and posters of your favorite rock star. Bring fun pillows, **cushions** and comfy bed **linens**. (The first time we ever heard of **XL twin sheets** was at college, and we've never heard of them since then!) Most of all, have fun with **upcycling**. **Amaze** your friends with your **creative** genius as you make bookshelves out of **cinder blocks**, and make lamps out of . . . well, *you* figure it out!

After freshman year you may decide not to live in the dorm. There are plenty of options! **Suites** are groups of rooms that several students share, with a **living room**, a few bedrooms, and a few bathrooms. Apartments have several rooms, like suites, but they also have a kitchen, so you can show your friends your **gourmet** cooking skills. (Hey, invite us on spaghetti night!) If you have decided to join a fraternity or sorority, you may be able to live in the frat (or sorority) house. Some students may find a place in town where they want to live. Apartments and frat houses may be on-campus or off-campus, but wherever you live, the most important thing is to be respectful of your neighbors!

THINK ABOUT IT

Is this your first time living away from home? Are you excited? Nervous? When you lived at home, did you share a room with your brother or sister? Now that you're an adult, how do you feel about sharing a dorm room with someone you don't know very well? Uh-oh, wait a minute—PLEASE don't tell us this will be your first time *doing your own laundry*, haha!

LANGUAGE SPOT: PHRASAL VERBS—LITERAL AND IDIOMATIC

Want to sound more natural when you speak English? OF COURSE YOU DO! And that got us thinking about phrasal verbs. Phrasal verbs are really common in informal English. They're verbs and particles (usually prepositions or adverbs) that work together to change the meaning of the verb. Relax—it sounds more complicated than it is! English speakers use phrasal verbs all the time, but trust us—you will probably never meet an English speaker who knows what a particle is! Just know that these verb phrases work together to make one meaning.

Got it?

Okay, then let's take a closer look. It's really important to **get the hang of** phrasal verbs if you want to understand and speak like a native.

There are two types of phrasal verbs: (1) the easy ones; and (2) the tricky ones! HAHA!

- *Literal* is the name for the easy ones. They're simple to understand because they mean exactly what they say.

    ◊ **Look for:** search for something/someone
    *Ugh, I've lost my glasses! Can you help me **look for** them please?*

- *Idiomatic* (or figurative, abstract, or metaphorical, depending on which grammar book you have—HA!) phrasal verbs are trickier, because it's impossible to figure out the meaning just by knowing the individual words. (Hey—"figure out"! That's another phrasal verb!)

    ◊ **Get over:** recover from an illness
    *It's taking so long to **get over** the flu. I feel like I've been sick for weeks!*

◊ **Get over:** feel happier after something bad has happened
*I know you feel sad that your girlfriend doesn't want to see you anymore, but after some time you'll **get over** it, and you'll find someone else.*

- Ha, and just to make things even more confusing, sometimes the same verb and particle can have BOTH a *literal* AND an *idiomatic* meaning.

    ◊ **Pick up:** lift something off a surface (literal)
    *Tell the baggage handler to be careful when he **picks up** your bag. It's really heavy! (What the heck did you pack?)*

    ◊ **Pick up:** to learn something informally (idiomatic)
    *Does American slang seem hard to understand? Don't worry— you'll **pick** it **up** in no time!*

TRY IT!

You heard a lot about *filling in* information at orientation. Take a look at these phrasal verbs with *fill*. Are they *literal* or *idiomatic*? Answers are on page 226.

- **fill in:** complete the items in a form with information
(1) _____
*Thanks for filling out this form, but you forgot to **fill in** the space for your phone number!*

- **fill out:** complete the form with information (2) _____
(yes! fill in! fill out! ALMOST the same, but not quite! hahaha, English!)
*Great! Thanks for filling in your phone number. Now the form is completely **filled out**!*

- **fill in:** give someone information about a problem or event
(3) _____
*Oh no! I can't go to the Art Club orientation meeting tonight. Will you **fill** me **in** tomorrow?*

- **fill out:** add weight; get fatter (4) _____
*Everyone noticed that the celebrity's cheeks had **filled out**. I think she had some **work** done!*

- **fill up:** put as much of something into a container as it can hold (5) _____
  *I want to **fill up** the tank with gas before we leave on our road trip. Mom is always saying, "Don't **fill up** on cookies! We're having dinner soon!"*

- **fill in for:** do a job in place of someone else (6) _____
  *The president can't make it to the meeting, so her assistant will **fill in for** her and make the announcements.*

Having fun? Well, let's *put in* a little more effort and *look at* a few more phrasals!

- **Put down:** put something on a surface (7) _____
  *I just can't **put down** this book, it's so much fun to read!*

- **Putdown:** something that makes someone feel silly, embarrassed, or offended (8) _____
  *What a **putdown**! Sally told me even a kindergartner is better at math than I am!*

- **cut off:** drive right in front of another car very suddenly (9) _____
  *Watch out for that silver car! The driver just **cut off** two cars in front of us.*

- **cut off:** stop the supply of something (10) _____
  *While they fixed the broken pipe in the street, the water company **cut off** water to the whole neighborhood.*

DIALOGUE: AUDIO TRACK 6

Roommates!

HE: Hey, hi! You must be my daughter Mary's roommate! Eleanor isn't it? . . . It's so nice to meet you **in person**!

SHE: Yes, that's me. I'm really glad to meet you too, Mr. Crawley. Mary told me all about her family in her emails. How was the drive from Ohio?

HE: It was actually fun. We listened to a **bunch** of interesting **podcasts** . . . I'm afraid Mary wasn't very impressed with my music. But I guess you didn't drive here from Beijing!

SHE: Ha, no, those oceans can be a little problem for the car! But I had a great flight. The weather was perfect, and I had a window seat.

HE: Great! That's such a long trip—I'm sure you must be exhausted. Hey, by the way, I was wondering about your name. Eleanor doesn't sound like a traditional Chinese name.

SHE: No, actually my name is Yu-Ching, but sometimes Americans aren't sure how to pronounce it. Eleanor is pretty easy for everyone to say. And I like it!

HE: I like it too. Okay, well, Mary will be back soon. She and her mom just went downstairs to get a soda. My job is to help figure out the room. So, do you have a preference for either side?

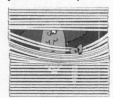

SHE: Well, unless Mary has a preference, I'd like the window side. When I'm studying, I like to look out the window.

HE: Of course—window seat on the plane . . . I should have figured! Well that's perfect. Mary always says the window is too **distracting** for her when she studies. She says she can't **concentrate** because she's too busy watching what's going on outside! So, can I help you get your stuff organized? Hey where is all your stuff?

SHE: Ha, I was only allowed to bring one suitcase on the plane. It looks like Mary is pretty organized though. She's brought all her towels and **bedding**. She's **set**!

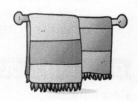

HE: Well, it was easy for her because we could pack everything in the car. She did most of the shopping at home with her mom. But I'm sure she'll be happy to go shopping with you, if you need stuff.

SHE: I do need lots of stuff. The Orientation team said there's a great **bed and bath** store at a local **strip mall**. They've arranged for buses all afternoon from the Student Center . . . and I think the next one leaves in about 20 minutes. I'm definitely going. If I don't, I'll be sleeping on a **bare mattress**!

HE: Oh, hey, here they come now. I'm sure Mary would love to take a break from unpacking . . . and she's always **up for** shopping!

SHE: Perfect!

YOUR TURN!

Based on the previous sections, decide if each is a good idea or a bad idea. Write *Good* or *Bad*. Answers are on page 227.

1. Make sure you know the rules of the residence hall. _____

2. Paint your dorm room your favorite vibrant color. _____

3. Wait until move-in day to meet your roommate. _____

4. Live off-campus so you can party all night long. _____

5. Review all the fire safety information and don't have cooking appliances in your room. _____

6. Ask your roommate which bed he or she would prefer. _____

7. Leave your shower supplies and towels in the hall bathroom. _____

8. If you hear a fire alarm, get out of the building immediately. _____

9. Wait for the university to tell you what dorm you'll be living in. _____

10. Commuter students should spend time on campus, doing things with other students. _____

BY THE WAY . . .

For safety reasons, all residence halls have secure entrances. You must be a student assigned to that dorm in order to get into the building. This doesn't mean that you can't have visitors, but you will need to follow the procedures that your dorm has in place. Are you lucky enough that your sister is coming for a visit? Yay! Most places will allow overnight guests for a short time, but be sure to check the rules for your dorm. Oh, and by the way . . . DON'T LOSE your room key or swipe card! If you do, you'll have to pay big bucks to replace it!

VOCABULARY

- **absolutely:** completely
- **ache:** pain, hurt
- **amaze:** surprise; shock
- **attract:** make someone want to do something
- **bare mattress:** the cushion part of the bed—without any sheets or coverings
- **bathrobe:** a comfy, fluffy coat you wear after a bath or shower
- **bed and bath:** a store or section of a store selling supplies for . . . yes, the bedroom and bathroom!
- **bedding:** sheets, blankets, pillows, and things to make a bed comfortable
- ⓘ **before you know it:** quickly
- **blast:** play something very, VERY loudly
- ⓘ **bookworm:** someone who likes to read
- ⓘ **bunch:** a lot
- **career:** profession; the job you want to do for a very long time
- **certainly:** surely; definitely; no question
- **cinder block:** a square made of cement used in building
- **concentrate:** focus; think only about what you're working on
- ⓘ **comfy:** comfortable
- **common area:** a place on a college campus where many students meet, like living or dining areas
- **commuter:** someone who travels for work or school
- **course load:** number of courses taken at one time
- ⓘ **crank up:** make the sound very loud
- **creative:** able to think of something unusual, or find an interesting way to make something useful
- **cushion:** a large square made of soft material to make a chair more comfortable
- **distracting:** making it difficult to concentrate; taking your attention away from your work
- ⓘ **dorm:** dormitory, residence hall
- **dynamic:** very active; energetic
- **enforced:** regulated; checked to be sure something is obeyed
- **evacuate:** leave a place quickly in an emergency; make a place empty
- **exemplary:** fantastic, an excellent example

- **field:** area of study
- **fitness center:** building to go and exercise; exercise gym
- **fluffy:** thick and soft
- **forbidden:** not allowed!
- ⓘ **fridge:** refrigerator; the place you put your food to keep it cool
- **full-time:** working the full number of hours a week, typically 40
- ⓘ **get the hang of something:** learn how to do something
- ⓘ **go off:** make a sound; make an alarm-noise
- **go away to school:** leave home to live at college (college is often called *school* in the U.S.)
- **gourmet:** delicious and high quality; fancy (food)
- **habit:** something that you do all the time as part of your everyday living
- **high-rise:** a very tall building
- ⓘ **hop:** jump
- **housing:** the places where people live
- **how else:** in what other way?
- **in person:** face to face
- ⓘ **juggle:** do many things at the same time; multi-task
- **lifestyle:** the way someone likes to live
- **linens:** sheets, tablecloths, and other fabrics to make the home more beautiful and comfortable
- **living room:** room where people sit together to talk or watch TV
- **move-in day:** the first day at the college, when all the students bring all their stuff to their new rooms
- **multi-task:** do many things at the same time
- **non-traditional:** not typical (like a student who is much older and may be working, or have a family)
- **option:** choice
- **outstanding:** excellent
- **part-time:** working less than the full number of hours a week (maybe 20 instead of 40)
- ⓘ **party animal:** someone who loves going to parties . . . lots and lots of parties!
- **podcast:** an audio program for your electronic device
- ⓘ **pooch:** dog
- **procedure:** process of doing something
- **roommate:** someone you share a room with
- **safety feature:** what keeps something from being dangerous

- ⓘ **to be set:** prepared; ready
- • **sheet:** thin cloth fitted to a bed; people sleep between two of them
- • **slippers:** comfy, fluffy shoes you wear inside your home
- • **smoke-free:** no smoking allowed
- ⓘ **stick around:** stay
- • **strip mall:** an outside mall
- • **student body:** the entire population of students at a school
- • **suite:** group of rooms with a kitchen and bathroom
- • **top priority:** most important thing
- ⓘ **toss:** throw; put something into the trash
- • **twin:** a small bed for one person; there are often two of them (twins!) in a dorm room
- ⓘ **up for:** be interested in doing something
- • **upcycle:** reuse an item to make something different and better
- • **XL:** for college bed sheets, this means e<u>X</u>tra <u>L</u>ong; in most other uses, it means extra large
- ⓘ **work:** plastic surgery

USE YOUR WORDS!

Look at these adjectives from the previous section. Add the correct one to the sentence. Answers are on page 227.

comfy	fluffy
creative	full-time
dynamic	gourmet
distracting	non-traditional
exemplary	outstanding

1. Hey, come on over for dinner tonight! I just plan to order pizza. There won't be any _____ food . . . unfortunately, ha!

2. I think I'll take a photography class. I have some different ideas after seeing my friend's _____ pictures of flowers in the rain.

3. It's hard to work _____ and take classes at night, but I know I'll be glad I did it when I have that college degree!

4. My roommate likes to listen to music while she studies. Not me! I find it too _____ and I can't concentrate on reading.

5. *RRRRRIIIIINNNNNNNGGGGGG!!!!!!* Noooooo, it can't be time to wake up yet! My bed feels so warm and _____ that I could stay here all day.

6. Well done, Tom! You did an _____ job on this assignment! A+!

7. You'll love this fancy restaurant. The food is excellent, and the service is

_____ .

8. Most of the people in my class are typical college students, but there's one amazing _____ student. She's 65 years old, and she's studying for a degree in math. WOW!

9. I chose this school because the campus is so _____ . There's energy and excitement everywhere!

10. I got some _____ purple cushions to make my chair comfortable and colorful.

SEND HELP!

Mail Center

Whew! Slow down and take a breath . . .

You've got it! You've settled in to your new **living quarters**, and you're getting to know your roommates or **suitemates**. Fun! College life in the U.S. is exciting, but it sure seems like there's a lot to know, doesn't it? Ha, and we're not even talking about the **coursework**! Trust us—you'll get the hang of everything faster than you think.

For now, you've got lots of places to go and lots of things to do . . . And we're pretty sure you're also thinking a lot about friends and family **back home**. This brings us to: THE MAIL CENTER! Most schools have a **central** post office on campus for mail. This is where to go to buy stamps, mail letters, and pick up **packages**. You can get all the information you need about postage rates (how much it costs to send stuff) and paperwork you may need for international mail. Sure, you use email all the time, but you can't get (or send!) a pretty package in email. (Well, not yet, ha!) Think about it—Isn't it fun to get a card from home with funny drawings by your **little** brother? Don't you love to open a package wrapped in pretty paper and find a gift that only your crazy friend at home would choose? And how about that really cool thing you bought online? MAIL!

In the old days, the Mail Center was the place for letters—letters from home, and letters to family and friends. Yes, letters! On paper! Written with a pen! Letters looked something like this:

	Dear Mom and Dad,
	Things are good at college. Please SEND MONEY!
	Love, Rusty

Yes, the letters were **short and sweet**, especially from our brother, Rusty. He checked for mail every day, hoping for a **reply** with news from home. Rusty's letter wasn't exactly what Mom and Dad were hoping for, but they were so happy to get *any* mail from their darling new college student that they sent a letter back **right away**. (And yes, they usually **enclosed** a check, ha!)

	Dear Rusty,
	Dad and I were so happy to get your letter!
	But you didn't tell us very much about school!
	Did you register for your classes yet? Is your roommate nice and quiet like you? What activities have you signed up to do? How is your class schedule? Do you have enough sweaters? Have you met your professors yet? How is the food? Are you eating enough vegetables? I hope you're not eating a lot of junk food! Please write back and tell us all about your exciting new college life. We want to hear about EVERYTHING!
	Love, Mom
	P.S. Enclosed is a check. Dad said you probably need it for books. Then he laughed.

On his next **trip** to the Mail Center, Rusty was excited to see that there was something in his mailbox. MAIL! Sure, it was great to get a letter from home, but haha—it was *really* great to get a *check* from home! After all, doesn't *everyone* need a little extra cash for fun stuff? Oh yeah, and . . . um . . . for books . . . of course. A few days later Rusty wrote a reply, brought it to the Mail Center, bought a stamp, and put his letter in the mailbox.

	Dear Mom and Dad,
	Thanks for the check. Everything is good! But I'll probably **run out of** money by next week.
	Love, Rusty

Yay—MAIL!

STUDENT BANKING

So you checked your mail, and SURPRISE! Aunt Isabel sent you a check! And of course you still have some money you brought from home. You sure don't want to walk around carrying a big wad of cash all the time . . . so . . . let's talk about *banking*. There are plenty of options. Trust us—*everyone* wants to help you with that wad of cash! Banks just love to offer credit cards and other services to students. Hmm . . . Could it be that they like to charge fees? Or that they hope you'll think your **shiny new** credit card is magic money that never has to be repaid? (Remember all those interest charges the banks like to collect from you!) And, of course, we know you remember exactly where you put that banking information you got at orientation . . . *right*? Ha!

Okay, we're here to make things nice and easy for you. Here it is: the most important thing about banking that you need to remember is one beautiful little word: FREE! Yes, FREE! Look for accounts that don't have a monthly **maintenance fee**. (Free!) Of course, you'll need to have money to put into the account, but choose one that has a low **minimum balance requirement** . . . or none. (Free!) Be sure the account gives you a (Free!) debit card to use. Of course, there should be no **online banking** or money transfer fees. (Free!) And, if you have your account with them, just about every bank allows you to use their ATMs with no fees. (Free!) But remember this: If you use an ATM at a bank where you *don't* have an account, that bank will let you withdraw the money using your card . . . BUT . . . that bank will charge you a fee. (On the screen you will need to **confirm** that you agree to their fee, or **cancel** the transaction.) And, guess what? Your bank, where you DO have an account, will ALSO charge a fee, just because you used another bank! (Definitely NOT FREE!)

There's one more thing to think about. Most accounts will let you choose to have **overdraft protection**. This sounds like a great idea . . . until you look at it carefully. Think about going to your favorite **upscale** store. (Okay, it's *our* favorite store, but haha, a girl can dream.) You've **picked out** the perfect **designer cashmere** sweater to **go with** your new jeans. You take it to the **cash register**. The cashier takes your debit card and **rings up** the purchase. $350! A **buy**! A **bargain**! A **steal**! A **deal**! You get back to the dorm, put on that fabulous sweater, check yourself in the mirror, and check your account on the phone. SURPRISE! You didn't have enough money in your account to cover the sweater! Oopsie! The bank transferred money from your overdraft account into your debit account. Oh, are you thinking, "That was so **thoughtful** and nice of them!"? Haha, well, yes, they transferred *your own* money from one account into another account so you could buy that fabulous designer cashmere . . . but guess what? They also added on a big fat fee! Your **gorgeous** sweater cost a heck of a lot more than you thought! And that, ladies and gentlemen, is how overdraft protection works. The **alternative** isn't pretty, but it will **avoid** those big fees. If you choose NOT to have overdraft protection, and you don't have enough money in the account to cover that sweater, the cashier will **process** the card, then probably say, "I'm sorry. Your card was **declined**." Oops! No cashmere for you until you **deposit** more **funds** into your account. I guess we know who will be going to the Mail Center today! "Dear Mom. Please send a check." Haha!

Just about every college has a bank office or ATM on campus, but that doesn't mean you must choose that bank. Research different bank services. Be sure there is an ATM nearby. Look for . . . FREE! And don't forget that there are online banks, too. **Do your homework**!

DISABILITY SUPPORT SERVICES

Federal and state laws require colleges to provide help to students with special needs so that they can join in all parts of the college experience. Colleges *want* everyone to succeed, and to be happy and comfortable on campus and in classes. To make sure that they meet the needs of anyone with a **disability**, colleges have a Disability Support Services Office. If you have any type of disability—health, psychological, physical (**mobility**, visual, hearing, or another), or any learning difference—this office will help you with the process of getting **accommodations** that you need to be successful. The office will advise you about what **documentation** you need, and they will help you arrange an accommodation with your instructor. Examples of special help are: extra time or a quiet area for taking tests, or use of **assistive technology**. Whatever assistance you need, be sure to check with the Disability Services Office—it's there for you!

THINK ABOUT IT

We know what you're thinking . . . Mail is a lot easier like this:

Sure, email and texting are faster and easier, but what about that feeling of going to your mailbox and finding . . . **snail mail**?! Have there been days when you've even been happy to get **junk mail**? Ha, maybe it's just us, but we've had days when we even read the grocery store flyer **cover to cover**! Yay, mail!

BY THE WAY . . .
As you know, there's a limit on the amount of money you're allowed to bring into the country. Boo! And although you can make payments (hello, tuition!) by credit card, there's usually a **daily limit** (and a maximum **credit limit**!) on credit. What does this mean to you? "Hello, Mom and Dad? Send money!" Mom and Dad can do a **wire transfer** of money from their bank at home to your bank at school. Of course there will be...FEES, but it's a safe way to get the money you need. Be very careful about businesses known as "check-cashing" places—many of them charge *very* high fees, and they are not as safe as banks.

LANGUAGE SPOT: EXPRESSIONS WITH *TAKE*

Let's talk about *take*. We took a look at phrasal verbs—verbs that go together with prepositions or adverbs. But there are lots of other verbs that just always go together with other words (often nouns) in English. (Sometimes the **Grammar Police** (ha!) will have different names for some of these: *collocations* or *set expressions*.) We like to call them *words that go together*. We don't care what they're called, but native speakers use them all the time. Have fun!

- **take notes:** Write down the most important information someone is saying
- **take a test:** No matter *how* you phrase this, NO ONE likes to do it. HA!
- **take (your) time:** Slow down! There's no need to do this quickly.
- **take a break:** It's time for a rest!
- **take a nap:** sleep for a short time
- **take a walk:** enjoy going by foot
- **take a walk/hike!:** funny (or sometimes rude) way to say *Go away!*
- **take a bite:** enjoy a taste of some food—especially someone else's food!
- **take care of:** help, watch over, protect someone or something
- **take care of:** do, complete, or manage a task or situation

And, our personal favorite: **takes the cake**! This can sometimes mean the best of everything, but it's commonly used to mean the opposite—"Wow. That is *really* bad!" Here's an example:

"My roommate had a loud party in the room last night, and I was trying to study for a test. And then she was angry at *me* because she woke up as I was getting ready for class this morning."

"WOW! I've heard of bad roommate behavior, but that really **takes the cake!**"

TRY IT!

Can you choose the best expression with *take* for the following situations? *Take your time.* **Answers on page 228.**

1. No baseball game for me this weekend. I have too many things to _____ before classes begin Monday.

2. Hey, it's a perfect spring day! Let's _____ to the park.

3. I really want a dog, but my schedule is too crazy for me to _____ a pet.

4. Exam time! The students were exhausted from studying all day. They decided to _____ and order in a pizza. Nice plan, kids!

5. It's really important to _____ in class; they will help you remember the important stuff when you have to (6.) _____.

7. Start early when you have an essay to write. Then you can _____ and do a good job, and you won't have to hurry at the end.

8. Wow, that was a great lunch, but I ate way too much! I feel so sleepy that I think I'll just _____ .

9. My crazy friend Carlos wanted to _____ of my cheeseburger! I told him to (10.) _____! Go buy your own lunch, Carlos!

DIALOGUE: AUDIO TRACK 7

Taking Care of Things

HE: Hey, are you busy? Do you feel like taking a walk to the bank with me?

SHE: Hmm . . . well, actually I was thinking about taking a nap . . . I've been working on my project all afternoon, and I'm exhausted!

HE: PERFECT! If you've been working all day, then you *need* to take a break. But not a nap—not on a gorgeous sunny day like today.

SHE: Okay, you're right. I guess a walk would be nice on such a beautiful day. But why are we going to the bank?

HE: Because I went to the Mail Center this morning.

SHE: Wait, wait, wait . . . What the heck are you talking about?! We're going to the *bank* because you went to the *Mail Center*?

HE: I knew you'd understand! Haha! . . . No, I need to go to the bank because I *got mail*. And the mail was a nice little note from the university reminding me that my tuition payment is due.

SHE: And we're going to the bank because . . . you're planning to pay your tuition in cash? Pennies, maybe?

HE: HA—See, that is why I wanted you to come with me! You always make me laugh! No, I'm going to the bank to ask about the money my parents transferred into my account. And YES, I know I can do that online, but I also want to talk to a person about different kinds of accounts.

SHE: Okay. Hmm . . . but as long as we're going that way, I need to take care of something important too. It's on the way to the bank.

HE: Sure. What do you need to do?

SHE: I need to GET A CHOCOLATE ICE CREAM CONE at Sam's Sweets!

HE: HA! Okay, let's take care of that very important business first! But only if you'll let me take a bite!

YOUR TURN!

Can you answer these questions about the previous sections? Answers are on page 228.

1. Take a little test! How many times did you see an expression with *take* in the dialogue on the previous page? Take a look, and take your time before you answer. _____

2. Credit cards often have a set amount of money that you're allowed to charge on one single day. What's that expression?

_____

3. Tricky one: Some bank accounts will charge a fee unless you keep a certain amount of money in the account at all times. What is the expression for that amount? _____

4. In the old days, letters were written on paper! What's the expression for mail that goes through the post office to someone's home mailbox?
_____

5. What adjective is commonly used to talk about a younger brother or sister? _____

6. If you don't have enough money in your debit account, can you still use the card to make a purchase at a store? _____

7. If you don't have overdraft protection, what happens when you try to make a purchase? _____

8. If the ATM on campus isn't your bank's ATM, can you get cash there?
_____

9. Are students with disabilities limited to certain activities?
_____

10. Can anyone get extra time on a test if he/she asks the professor?
_____

BY THE WAY . . .

We just love acronyms! An acronym is a "word" made from the initials of other words. When you use the ATM, you're using an *Automated Teller Machine*. To use the ATM, you need your bankcard and your PIN—*Personal Identification Number*. APY—*Annual Percentage Yield*—is how much interest the bank will pay you to keep your money in a deposit account. (Ha, trust us—It's not much!) Here's one you hope you never see: NSF—*NON-SUFFICIENT FUNDS*! Hoo boy! That one means you didn't have enough money in the account to pay for what you wanted to buy, and you know what that means—FEES!

VOCABULARY

- **accommodation:** a change that allows someone with a special need to participate in an activity
- **alternative:** another choice
- **assistive technology:** equipment that allows someone with a special need to participate in an activity or to complete a task
- **avoid:** keep away from
- ⓘ **back home:** the country or city you come from
- ⓘ **bargain:** a really great price!
- ⓘ **buy:** a really great price!
- **cancel:** stop something from happening
- **cash register:** the machine that processes a sale
- **cashmere:** beautiful, fine, soft wool
- **central:** main; in a middle area
- **confirm:** say that you agree
- **coursework:** the stuff you're studying!
- **cover to cover:** every word of some printed material
- **credit limit:** the top amount of money the bank will allow you to charge
- **daily limit:** the top amount of money you're allowed to withdraw in one day
- ⓘ **deal:** a really great price!
- **decline:** say no; not accept
- **deposit:** put money in
- **designer:** person who styles beautiful things
- **disability:** a condition that limits someone's activities
- ⓘ **do your homework:** research everything about a subject!
- **documentation:** proof of something
- **enclosed:** inside something else (like a check inside a letter, ha!)
- **fee:** money charged for a service
- **funds:** money!
- ⓘ **go with:** match something else; be a part of something else
- **gorgeous:** really, really beautiful!
- ⓘ **Grammar Police:** Haha, people who tell others there is a little mistake in how they said or wrote something! (The people exist, but a Grammar Police group does NOT exist—only in fun!)

- **junk mail:** advertisements, catalogs, and menus that you didn't ask for
- ⓘ **little:** younger
- **living quarters:** housing
- **maintenance fee:** the money the bank charges for managing your account
- **minimum balance requirement:** the lowest amount of money you must keep in your account before the bank charges a fee
- **mobility:** ability to move
- **online banking:** checking all that money and bank stuff online! Also, banks that don't have buildings, only Internet accounts
- **overdraft protection:** system of taking money from another account to cover a purchase when you don't have enough money in the first account. There's a fee, ha!
- **package:** a box, parcel, or large envelope
- ⓘ **pick out:** choose
- **process:** do the steps to complete an action; the system or way of doing something
- **reply:** answer
- **right away:** NOW! immediately
- ⓘ **ring up:** process a sale at a store
- ⓘ **run out of (something):** use all of something so that nothing is left
- ⓘ **shiny new:** really, really new!
- ⓘ **short and sweet:** very brief and right to the important issue
- **snail:** a small, very, very, VERY slow creature that carries its shell house on its back!
- ⓘ **snail mail:** mail sent using the post office system
- ⓘ **steal:** a really, really good price!
- **suitemates:** the people who share your suite
- **thoughtful:** thinking about the feelings of others
- ⓘ **trip:** short journey, often used with tasks outside the house (a trip to the bank, a trip to the store . . .)
- **upscale:** fancy; expensive
- **wire transfer:** electronically sending money from one account to another

USE YOUR WORDS!

Match the informal words or expressions with a definition. Answers are on page 229.

a. younger

b. choose

c. match something else; be a part of something else

d. It's a really great price!

e. learn about something, or learn how to do something

f. an outing to do some tasks

g. process a sale at a store

h. very brief and right to the important issue

i. use something until there is no more left

j. research everything about a subject!

1. _____ trip

2. _____ do your homework

3. _____ ring up

4. _____ get the hang of

5. _____ little

6. _____ pick out

7. _____ run out of (something)

8. _____ It's a steal!

9. _____ go with

10. _____ short and sweet

FUN WITH IDIOMATIC EXPRESSIONS: Getting Started

- **off to a flying start:** a really good beginning
  *First day of classes . . . finished! First paper . . . started! I'm **off to a flying start**!*

- **start off on the right foot:** start doing something the right way in order to succeed
  *My instructor said I really **started off on the right foot** by seeing her during office hours to check on the assignment instructions.*

- **don't get me started:** Ugh, that's a topic that will get me annoyed!
  ***Don't get me started** on that politician! He is against everything I believe in!*

- **get rolling/get the ball rolling:** get something started
  *Okay guys, we really need to **get rolling** on this group project or it won't be finished on time.*
  *I'll **get the ball rolling** by reserving the computer lab for next week.*

- **on a roll:** having a lot of good luck or success
  *I can't believe it! I got an A on my first paper, an A on my test, and my parents just wired me some extra cash. I'm **on a roll** today!*

- **make a fresh start:** begin again in a new way
  *Last semester I was a party animal and my grades were not good. This semester I'm **making a fresh start**. I'm going to be a bookworm, study hard, and make great grades!*

- **start from scratch:** start from the beginning
  *Oh no! Somehow I deleted my file, and if I can't find it saved in the cloud I'll have to **start from scratch**.*

- **get going:** get started to go somewhere; start making progress on a project
  *Whoa, look at the clock! Let's **get going** or we'll be late for class! I'll **get going** on the paper after I take a nap.*

- **get it in gear:** Hurry up! Get energetic and get started!
  *If you don't **get it in gear** and start some research, you'll never get that paper finished.*

- **start out with:** begin with something or someone before a change
  *The club **started out with** 30 new people at orientation, but by the 4th meeting, there were only 12 new members who wanted to continue.*

TRY IT!

What expression from the list above works best in these sentences? You may need to change the form of the verb. Answers are on page 229.

1. I _____ with $200 in my wallet this morning, but I only have five bucks left after buying my textbooks!

2. I really need to _____ on this paper but I can't think of a good way to start.

3. This long lunch was great, but I need to _____ so I'm not late for my next class.

4. Yay! I got an A on my first paper in English. I'm _____!

5. Rats! This is another idea that just won't work. I'm going to throw out this plan and _____ !

JUST FOR FUN!

Rusty's dad was having lunch with a friend. His friend wanted to know what subjects Rusty is studying at school.

Friend: What's Rusty taking at college?

Rusty's Dad: He's taking . . . ALL MY MONEY!

TIP: Bumper Stickers

Come on, we know you've done it. Your friend is driving along and you say, "Hey, can you get a little closer? What is the little sign on that guy's car?" Welcome to the wild and **wacky** world of **bumper stickers**! Many Americans love to put these little signs on the back of their cars. Some show places a family (and car!) have visited: "This car climbed Mt. Washington!" Some show pride in a favorite college, or advertise something they like. "My dog **digs** his **vet**!" Some support an environmental **cause**: "Lights Off for Turtles" or "Save the Whales!" Around election time you'll see plenty of: "EDDIE MELLAN FOR PRESIDENT!" You can probably guess that our favorite bumper stickers are the funny ones. How about "My Other Car is a Lamborghini"? But our all-time favorite that makes us laugh every time is: "I may be slow, but I'm in front of you!"

TIP: The Scenic Route

We're sure you plan to do lots of traveling while you're in the U.S. Great! There are plenty of really cool places to go, and there are two ways to get there: the quick **route**, and the **scenic** route. If you enter the **destination** into your GPS or maps app, you'll get optional routes. Our advice: If you have the time, avoid the highway traffic and take the local roads . . . It will take longer to get where you plan to go, but you may find an America you never expected along the **back roads**. Haha, just be sure you stay ON whatever road you choose!

Explore! The best adventures are the ones you didn't plan.

 ## ROAD TRIP: Hilton Head Island, South Carolina

Sand, sea . . . more sand and more sea! What could be better? Want a lazy vacation? This is the place for you! Want an active vacation? This is the place for you! Yes, at Hilton Head you can sit in the sun on the beach or you can do tons of fun sports . . . like **jet skiing** and sailing . . . it's all here. Um, did we say *fun* sports? Ha, they may be fun for you, but we'll be sitting on the beach, watching *you* do the watersports!

But we're not the only creatures that love Hilton Head's beaches. Early in May, loggerhead turtles begin nesting in the sand. Besides being really cool, these turtles are a **threatened** species, and local people are very careful about protecting them. It's really interesting to see the turtles' **nests** on the beach, but touching them is forbidden. In fact, local rules even forbid lights near the beach at night, because the light discourages nesting. If you're really lucky, you may see a turtle come up to lay its eggs. Cool! What you will *definitely* see are bumper stickers that say, "Lights Off for Turtles." It's a good reminder that everyone can help in the **conservation** effort.

While you're **exploring** on the beach, you can also look for horseshoe crabs. Sometimes you may see a live one, but very often you'll just see their big, hard shells. And trust us, you'll know if you step on one in the water—OUCH! Which reminds us . . . if you decide to take a swim, watch out for jellyfish! They're hard to see in the water, but WOW, you'll feel them! Jellyfish **stings** are really painful! Good luck!

Did you sign up for the Turtle Tour? Do you love seeing animals **in the wild**? At Hilton Head you can take a boat tour and watch dolphins swim right up to the side of the boat. Ha, but don't try to **pet** one—they may seem playful, but they can still take a big **bite** out of you! And speaking of *teeth* . . . Don't miss the ALLIGATORS! You definitely do NOT want to get too close to one of these **bad boys**. They may look kind of sleepy and lazy, but WHAM! They're lightning fast, and they think *you* look delicious, ha.

Hilton Head Island is one of many great beach resorts in the U.S. There's something for everyone! Hey, look for us . . . sitting on the beach, of course.

☑ QUICK FACTS

☑ How many states make up the *United States*? Take a look at the American flag! How many stars do you see? Okay, no need to count, we'll tell you. There are 50 stars . . . one for each of the 50 states!

☑ Hmm . . . That takes care of the stars . . . What about the **stripes** on the flag? Did you count them? There are 13. These represent the 13 **original colonies**.

☑ An informal name for the American flag is . . . the Stars and Stripes!

ANY QUESTIONS?

- What do we mean by *original colonies*? Well, it's a very long story, but the United States began as a group of colonies of Great Britain. When the colonies became an independent country, the new country became the United States of America.

- Okay, so what were the 13 original colonies that got the whole thing started? Connecticut, Delaware, Georgia, Maryland, Massachusetts, New Hampshire, New Jersey, New York, North Carolina, Pennsylvania, Rhode Island, South Carolina, and Virginia.

VOCABULARY

- **back road:** local road going through countryside and small towns
- ⓘ **bad boys:** things that are a problem
- **bite:** cut with teeth OUCH!
- **bumper stickers:** message on paper on the back of a car
- **cause:** an important issue or belief
- **colony:** a settlement of people ruled by a larger country
- **conservation:** protection; keeping safe
- **destination:** place you are going to
- ⓘ **dig:** really like (Hey, this was a popular Woodstock word!)
- **explore:** investigate while traveling
- **in the wild:** in the natural environment
- **jet ski:** small "boat" one person sits on
- **nest:** place where birds and some other animals make their home and lay eggs
- **original:** first; beginning
- **original colonies:** the first European settlements in the U.S.
- **pet:** touch gently
- **route:** the way to get from one place to a destination
- **scenic:** pretty, with very nice views
- **sting:** sharp pain
- **stripes:** lines
- **threatened:** in danger; an animal species in need of protection
- **vet:** animal doctor; so much easier to say than *veterinarian*!
- ⓘ **wacky:** silly; crazy in a funny way

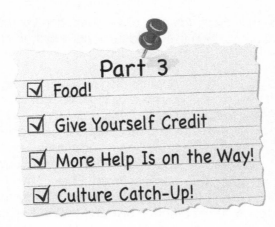

Part 3

- ☑ Food!
- ☑ Give Yourself Credit
- ☑ More Help Is on the Way!
- ☑ Culture Catch-Up!

FOOD!

Meal Plans

Yay, it's time to talk about . . . FOOD! The only thing we like better than talking about food is *eating* food. And the only thing better than eating food is eating *free* food, ha! We're sorry to tell you this, but you had your free food at orientation—now it's time to buy lunch. Hmm, well, maybe . . .

Most colleges require incoming freshmen to buy a **meal plan**. That's good news AND bad news! The good news is that you don't have to worry about buying your meals every day. You already bought them when you paid for the meal plan! The bad news is that you may **need a college degree** to figure out all the different meal plans available, haha! A meal plan simply means that you pay **in advance** for the semester, and the meals you choose are covered. Instead of paying at the cash register after you select your food, you simply swipe your card, and the cost of that meal is deducted from your account. But there are tons of meal plan options—you really need to do your homework to find the best one for you.

Some schools offer the option of three meals a day. That may sound like a good (and very expensive!) idea, but think about YOUR eating habits. Do you like to sleep in if you don't have an early class? Then you probably won't want breakfast every day. Will you be off-campus a lot during lunch or dinner times? You may prefer to eat in town. If you don't usually have three full meals a day at home, then this could be your Freshman 15 plan! NOT a good idea!

Another plan may offer some meals in certain campus dining halls, but allow you a "Dining Dollars," "Mascot Money," or "Campus Cash" account. These accounts (that often have cute names!) allow you to use some of your plan money to eat at any place that accepts those "bucks," even off-campus. Our local university allows students to use their meal plan account to shop at the **farmers' market** on campus! Learn about all the meal plans before you choose one. Here's why it's really important to find out exactly how each plan works: If you don't **use up** all your meal credits, many places will NOT **refund** you the money for the meals you **skipped**!

But "how many meals?" isn't the only question you need to ask. Are you a **picky eater**? (Ha, not us!) Be sure to find out what kind of food options you will get with each plan. Do you have certain **dietary restrictions**? Do you want a **vegetarian** or **vegan** menu? Find out your choices *before* you select a meal plan. It's a really good idea to check online, or email Food Services at the college and ask for **sample** menus. Most Food Services managers do a pretty good job of **keeping up with** food **trends** that are popular with students. A dining hall usually has many "**stations**"—places serving different kinds of food. In the same large space, you can grab a **slice** at the pizza **counter** while your friend orders fish tacos at the Mexican station. Another friend may order a sandwich at the **deli** counter, while we order a salad at the **salad** station. HAHA, only kidding! We don't want a salad—we're over at the dessert station ordering an ice cream **sundae**! Does everything look delicious? Great! If not, and if your school requires students to get a meal plan, think about getting the smallest plan you can. Just be sure to set aside money to cover your *non-plan* meals! Don't **panic**! You won't starve! There are usually lots of **inexpensive** places to eat around most college campuses.

FOOD TRUCKS

Ha, who needs dining halls and student cafés? And (unless it's required and you like the **convenience**) who needs a meal plan? If your school is large, or if it's in a big city or town, you'll have plenty of dining choices off-campus. In fact, one of the most popular dining options for students, faculty, local business people, and **foodies** is . . . the FOOD TRUCK! Food trucks are so popular that there are often **lines** of people waiting. Lots of trucks serving all kinds of food **park** right around college campuses—and they're not just for students. You may be standing in line right behind your chemistry professor! The food is excellent, and the international **cuisine** choices are endless— from Mexican and Italian dishes to Vietnamese and Greek. And, as your chemistry professor certainly knows, local rules require a food truck to be as clean as a restaurant. **Health inspectors** check them **regularly**, and there are very strict rules about cleanliness and food preparation.

You're probably already familiar with vendors selling street food, but in U.S. cities there are just as many selling fancy gourmet food. Sometimes professional chefs may try out new **recipes**, and a beginning chef may start out cooking on a food truck. If his cuisine becomes really popular . . . *Poof!* It can be the start of a successful restaurant career! In fact, one of our favorite movies is about a famous chef who is unhappy with the rules and limitations at the restaurant where he works. So he quits his job and starts cooking all the things he has a **passion** for . . . on a food truck. It becomes hugely popular, and he is happy to be doing what he loves . . . with his family joining in! (Okay, we don't recommend that you quit your job to go cook on a truck . . . but it's an interesting idea, ha!)

What do you feel like eating? Food truck menu choices are endless. Of course there are tons of **ethnic** specialties, but other chefs **come up with unique** ideas about simple American classics like **grilled cheese**. (If you haven't had a grilled cheese sandwich yet, stop reading right now and go try one!) Students have favorite chefs and food trucks, and they often use social media to find out where their favorite truck will be parked on a certain day. You do *not* want to miss the PB&J truck, ha! (We won't mention that our favorite is the caramel cupcake dessert truck . . . oops . . . we mentioned it.)

Whatever food you love, there's probably a truck selling it near school, and at a very good price. We don't always know who's cooking on the food trucks, but we sure do like the results. **Delish**!

CHAIN RESTAURANTS

So you and a few friends have decided to **splurge** on dinner. No meal plan selection today! No cafeteria! No food truck! You want to sit down at a casual, comfortable restaurant, order from a menu, and relax while a server brings your food. You're in luck! College towns are perfect locations for **sit-down chain restaurants**, because they're so popular with students . . . and their teachers! What is a chain restaurant? It's one of many restaurants with the same name, found in many different places, all owned by the same company. In a chain restaurant, the menu is usually the same in all locations. The **décor** is the same. The quality is the same. So what is a sit-down chain restaurant? Well, the most important **feature** is that you, um . . . *sit down*, relax, and wait for a server to take your order and deliver your delicious **fettuccine Alfredo**!

The prices at these chains are usually about the same everywhere. They're **pricier** than fast food, but you can usually find special deals. Look for **coupons** in the newspaper. Coupons have special codes that you can scan with your phone, or cut out of the paper to give the server at the restaurant. If you have a coupon you can get special prices for your dinner. Yay! And don't forget your student ID! If you don't have a coupon, and there isn't a student discount, just plan your dinner early! A lot of restaurants have an "Early Bird Special." If you go for dinner before 5:00, there are very inexpensive meal choices. Of course, that means you'll be hungry again at 11:00, haha, but then you can order a pizza for delivery to your dorm!

Fast food restaurants are also chain restaurants. (Come on—can you think of a fast food burger restaurant that's part of a chain?) But fast food chains are not relaxing, *sit-down* places. They may make great burgers, but you **place your order** and pay at a counter, then you bring your own tray to a table. Fast food restaurants aren't very fancy or relaxing for a special meal, but they're very inexpensive. Go on and splurge! No fast food tonight! Enjoy an evening at a sit-down restaurant. **Forget** the college meal plan tonight!

WHAT'S IN TO EAT?
(The Mom Version)

It's the classic American kid question, as soon as they're home from school! "Hey, Mom, **what's in** to eat? I'm starving!" We don't really think she's starving, but come on, doesn't everyone want an after-school snack? Um . . . YES! So what are all these kids eating? Well, if Mom **had her way**, the perfect snack would be fresh fruit or . . . **veggies**! We can picture it now—a plate of carrot and celery **sticks** topped with peanut butter. Vegetables and a great source of protein—what could be better? Raw vegetables are popular because . . . they're not junk food! A fancy word for a snack of raw vegetables is *crudités*. (Yes, it's French!) **Impress** your friends! The vegetables are cut up into pieces, and they're often served with a **dip**—some type of creamy sauce. Vegetables often found in a **snack tray** are carrots, celery, cucumbers, broccoli and cauliflower **florets**, and peppers. The dip gives a nice creamy taste.

But even Mom knows that sometimes a kid (or adult!) just needs a sweet snack. The most typical sweet after-school snack is: cookies and milk. And the most typical kind of cookie is: chocolate chip! A big glass of cold milk with some chocolate chip cookies is the perfect way to say, "Let's relax after all that hard work at school . . . and before all that hard work at homework!" (Don't ask us to explain chocolate chip cookies—you just have to try them yourself! Yum!)

Speaking of chocolate chip cookies . . . When Mom's little darling heads off to college, Mom likes to make sure he knows that the family back home is thinking of him. What better way to say, "Hey, we miss you!" than to send . . . a **care package**? Hey, Rusty, go check the Mail Center! You have a package. And it's not just any package . . . it's a *care package from home*! Believe us, that is good news not only for Rusty; it's great news for his roommates too! A care package is a box packed full of all kinds of goodies—packed so full that Rusty can't possibly eat it all—packed so full that everyone in nearby rooms will get to share. Hey, Rusty—HURRY! Get that package! Who can concentrate on studying when there's a big box of Mom's homemade chocolate chip cookies waiting in the Mail Center?

WHAT'S IN TO EAT?
(The Dorm Version)

Unless you're lucky enough to share Rusty's care package from home, there's a very good chance you'll be eating typical dorm snacks. What you need to know is that dorm snacks and dorm dinners are very often the same thing! I guess we should just call it "dorm-food." Are you thinking that dorm-food will be very similar to what a college student eats at home? NO! Okay, we're going to help you along and tell you the most famous items on the dorm-food **shopping list**. Think of it as the Junk Food Option of the College Meal Plan List. (Nooooo!!!!! We're **kidding**! Don't try to buy this meal plan at Food Services! You're **on your own** for the junk food plan!)

Do you like **noodles**? HA! *Everyone* loves noodles! **Ramen** noodles are really popular at college because, well, they're delicious . . . but also because they're so easy to prepare. Trust us: "easy to prepare" is probably one of the most important **factors** in meal selection at college. Okay, are you thinking of a bowl of ramen noodles in nice hot soup? Hmm. Maybe. But some students just like to eat them right out of the package! We're not kidding—they break the dry noodles into pieces and eat them as a salty snack, like chips. (We told you—"easy to prepare" is very popular!)

Another kind of "noodle" is macaroni, and another top dorm meal is **mac and cheese**. In fact, mac and cheese is popular just about everywhere in the U.S.—even at home! You can tell it's really popular, because everyone calls it by its **nickname** instead of its real name, which is *macaroni and cheese*. Ha, and that's pretty much the recipe right there: macaroni . . . with cheese (usually cheddar, a sharp, sometimes orange-colored cheese). But don't try this one **straight from** the package. Mac and cheese is definitely a cooked snack. But, like most popular cooked snacks, it comes in an instant . . . *easy to prepare* . . . package that you can **microwave**. YUM!

Of course, chips and salty snacks are everywhere on college campuses, and dorms are always full of the buttery smell of microwave popcorn. (Microwaves aren't allowed in dorm rooms, but they're provided in the kitchen, and in student **lounges** around campus.) The microwave may possibly be the most important college student device . . . after personal electronics! That buttery popcorn isn't the only snack, um, **popping up** in dorms. Don't forget about microwave pizza!

And if you're not in the mood for a hot or salty snack, a really popular junk food meal is **cereal**. Yes, *breakfast* cereal. Breakfast cereal for lunch, or snack, or . . . dinner in the dorm! Sugary, sweet, colorful breakfast cereal . . . with or without milk. Some students don't even worry about using a bowl—they buy small boxes of cereal and just pour the milk straight into the package. We are not making that up!

Dorm snacks! Don't tell Mom!

LET'S GO GROCERY SHOPPING

When you were living at home did the snacks and meals just **appear**—kind of like a Mom magic trick? We're sorry to tell you that if you want a snack at college, you'll have to get it yourself—and not by magic! You'll have to go **grocery** shopping. Yes, grocery shopping—that wonderful weekend activity that you either love or hate . . .

 Here's what we LOVE about grocery shopping:

- FREE SAMPLES in the deli **department**! Sure, you're there to buy some cheese, nice, thinly sliced roast beef, and freshly prepared potato or macaroni salad . . . But is there a kind of cheese you've never tried? Are you not sure if you'll like the honey-baked turkey? Ask to taste it. The worker will cut a slice for you to try. Free sample!

- PRODUCT DEMOS everywhere! Speaking of trying things and free samples . . . Weekends, when many people are shopping, are a great time for companies to introduce new products. You'll see tables throughout the store with a person doing a **demo**: preparing a special food item, and giving it away in little cups. Or maybe he is giving away packages of a new snack bar. The **demonstrator** shows you the new product, and the company hopes you'll love the free sample so much that you'll buy more. The demonstrator will probably give you a coupon too. Lots of times the new products are on sale—offered at a special price for a short time.

- BOGO! Yay—<u>B</u>uy <u>O</u>ne <u>G</u>et <u>O</u>ne (free!)! This is even better if the product is already on your shopping list. Say your favorite chocolate chip cookies are BOGO . . . That means you take home two packages of cookies, but you only pay for one. WooHoo! Of course, the bad news is that this means you will eat twice as many cookies as you should . . . or that you will be crowding your freezer with too much stuff until someone says, "There's no room in the freezer! Why are all these cookies in here?!" Oh wait. Maybe that's just us . . .

 Here's what we HATE about grocery shopping:

- THE WRONG LINE *every* time we shop! Come on, you know what we're talking about. You do your shopping, and you just want to get home. So you look at the lines for all the cashiers, and you check the **carts** of all the people on those lines, and you make a decision: THIS line is the one moving fastest. HA. Then it's almost your turn, and the person ahead of you is an **extreme couponer**. *NOOOOooooooo!!!!* An extreme couponer is someone we actually admire very much. It's a person who has researched and filed and printed out and cut out and saved and remembered coupons for *every product* she wants to buy. Then she gets to the cash register and the cashier has to scan every one of her *2 million coupons*! Okay, maybe it's not really 2 million, but you get the idea. By the time all of her coupons are subtracted from the total amount, the extreme couponer sometimes pays only a few dollars for hundreds of dollars' worth of items. Good-bye fast line. (But she sure saves lots of $$$$$!)

- THE EXPRESS LANE person who can't count . . . The **Express Lane** is for people in a hurry—people with just a few items to buy. (It's sometimes called the "speedy **checkout**.") Express lanes have big signs that say "10 items!" or "20 items!" HA! We may not be counting, but we can tell that the big cart FULL of groceries has too many items to be in this lane. It will be a not-so-speedy checkout! So we go to the . . .

- SELF-CHECKOUT! In the **self-checkout** aisle we scan and **bag** all our groceries ourselves. A perfect plan until . . . "Sorry, this register only accepts credit cards" and "Sorry, this register is not working" and "Sorry, there is an error. Please wait for the cashier." *Aaaarghhh!!!!!*

- RAIN CHECKS. Okay, **rain checks** are good and bad. Rain checks are coupons the store gives customers if the store runs out of something that's on sale that week. The rain check lets you buy the item later for the sale price. Rain checks are good, because if the store runs out of the product, you can use the rain check any other time. Rain checks are bad, because: (1) the store doesn't have the item *you want now*; (2) you have to remember *not to lose* the rain check; and (3) you have to remember to *bring* the rain check when you go shopping next time!

Love it, or hate it, everyone must go grocery shopping sometime! If you're like us, you enjoy walking down all the aisles, looking for yummy stuff that's *not* on your shopping list! But maybe you just want to go quickly into the store, buy the six items on your list, and get back home. If that's you, then just **head to** the **aisles** that have what you need.

Take a look at our handy guide to supermarket departments, and get shopping!

- PRODUCE: fresh fruits and vegetables
- DAIRY: milk, cheese, butter, and yogurt
- DELI: **prepared** salads and **cold cuts**. These are meats and cheeses that you order by the pound. The meats are **sliced**, as you want them, usually for sandwiches. "I'll have a quarter pound of **rare** roast beef, and a half pound of American cheese, sliced **thin**, please."
- MEATS: Fresh meats for cooking. Will you recognize all the types of meat you see? Good luck!
- SEAFOOD: Yes . . . *food* from the *sea*, ha. Fresh fish!
- BAKERY: Oh yeah, we love this one! Freshly baked bread, DONUTS, cookies, and cakes. Yum.
- FROZEN FOODS: vegetables, pizza, ice cream, and desserts. And of course, for the microwave cooks like us, there are frozen breakfast, lunch, and dinner meals that you can heat in the microwave. That's *our* kind of cooking!

Some American supermarkets are HUGE, but don't worry—you won't get lost, ha! Each aisle has a large sign that tells you what's in the aisle. (Look for us in the cookie aisle!)

FARMERS' MARKETS

Have you decided to amaze your friends (and family back home!) with your wonderful cooking skills? Are you looking for the freshest vegetables? Fresh pies, cakes, and homemade breads? Farmers' markets are a great place to find local herbs, cheese, jams, homemade pasta noodles, and baked goods. You can often find special spices and even ethnic foods. Big cities usually have markets in several places, often on weekends. Our local university has a small market once a week, right outside the bookstore, and students can use their dining plans to make purchases. Go on—**pick up** some fresh ingredients and have a party!

THINK ABOUT IT

Maybe it's just us, but we always notice the food in a new place. How different are meals in the U.S., compared to those in your country? For example, do people eat the same kinds of things at breakfast? Do **convenience stores** sell "scrambled egg and cheese on a bagel" as typical morning foods? Were you surprised to see many different ethnic food choices in American restaurants? What different typical foods have you tried? Which ones are your favorites? Is there something you "WILL NEVER EAT AGAIN!!!"? Have you shopped in a supermarket yet? Did you recognize everything? Haha—how many breakfast cereals did you find?

BY THE WAY . . .

While you're checking meal plans, be sure to ask about semester breaks. When school is closed, the dining halls are usually closed too. As an international student, you may be on campus even when there are no classes. Does the school have dining accommodations for international students? Are meals included for international students over breaks? Will all dining halls be open? If not, which dining hall will be open for you? Is there a special option for international students? Some colleges may provide an opportunity to share a holiday meal with an American family. That's a great way to experience both holiday foods *and* culture! You're sure to be an honored guest—your **hosts** want to know all about your culture too!

LANGUAGE SPOT: SIMILES AND METAPHORS

Language is always more interesting when there are fun ways to talk about things. Similes and metaphors are interesting ways to make comparisons. We can say, "It's fun," or we can say, "It's as much fun as a bunch of monkeys in art class." (We'll take the monkeys!) When we compare different things using the words *like* or *as*, we're using a *simile* ("*as* fun *as* . . . "). When we compare different things by saying one *IS* something else, we're using a *metaphor*. Here's an example: "I love that art class—it's always a party!" The art class isn't really a *party* (ha, we don't think so, anyway!), but to say just how much fun it is, we use a metaphor and say the class *IS* a party.

TRY IT!

Do you have a sweet tooth? We sure do! Here's a sweet simile and metaphor activity using idioms with the words *cookie*, *cake*, *candy*, and *pie*. Using these delicious idioms, complete the expressions on the next page. Then write whether each is a *simile* or a *metaphor*. Answers are on page 229.

- **smart cookie:** someone smart who thinks creatively in difficult situations

- **tough cookie:** someone very strict and demanding; someone able to overcome hard challenges

- **icing on the cake:** the very best thing among other good things; sometimes used to mean the opposite: the very worst thing among bad things

- **piece of cake:** really easy

- **have your cake and eat it too:** able to take advantage of something good

- **go/sell like hotcakes:** selling, or running out very fast (Okay, technically hotcakes are those sweet, round breakfast pancakes, but hey, they're CAKES!)

- **have a finger in every pie:** be involved in many things

- a kid in a candy **store:** someone really excited to have a choice of lots of things they love

- **taking candy from a baby:** very easy! (Hmm. The babies we know would make it very hard to take their candy, ha!)

- **pie in the sky:** a dream or hope that's not realistic

IDIOMS: SIMILE or METAPHOR

		Simile or Metaphor?
1.	The entire day was perfect, and his proposal was **the icing on the** _____.	
2.	She's a **smart** _____. When they missed the last bus, she opened an app on her phone to get a ride.	
3.	You can't go away for spring break AND catch up on your coursework. That's like **having your _____ and eating it too**.	
4.	I was so worried about the math test, but actually it was **a piece of _____**! I got an A.	
5.	Some people think calculus is hard, but for my roommate **it's as easy as taking _____ from a baby**.	
6.	The free cookies at orientation **went like _____**. I didn't even get ONE!	
7.	He thinks he can get into law school with his low grades, but that's just _____ **in the sky** thinking.	
8.	That professor is a **tough _____**! She gives more homework than all my other teachers combined, and she won't take ANY excuses.	

	Simile or Metaphor?
9. He has a **finger in every** _____. He's involved in lots of student clubs, and he volunteers for three community groups.	
10. I was starving! When I got to the food truck, I was like a **kid in a** _____ **store** with all the choices!	

The Express Lane

HE: I knew it, I just knew it. The store is **packed**! Where are all these people coming from?

SHE: Oh, come on. You knew it would be crowded. It's Saturday! Everybody goes shopping on Saturday.

HE: Right, I get it. But this is even more crowded than usual. What the heck is going on?

SHE: Wait a minute . . . Wasn't the big food truck festival today? Maybe people are excited to try their favorite food truck's recipes. Maybe they're **stocking up** on **ingredients**.

HE: Wait, WHAT?! WE MISSED THE FOOD TRUCK FESTIVAL?!

SHE: Oh. You wanted to go? Oh well . . .

HE: Oh man, and they were giving the VENDY awards today . . . and WE MISSED IT!

SHE: What the heck are the VENDY awards, and why do you care?

HE: Are you kidding? Do we even live in the same city? The VENDY awards—for best food trucks!

SHE: I guess this means you have a favorite . . .

HE: You bet I do! I was hoping my favorite caramel-double-fudge-walnut-cream-chocolate-raspberry-cake truck would win the Best Dessert Truck award!

SHE: Do they have an award for a Get-This-Crazy-Guy-to-a-Gym-Fast Truck?

HE: Haha, very funny. Hey, I don't only eat junk food. Yes, I voted for the Best Dessert Truck, but I also voted for the Best Healthy Eating Truck, too.

SHE: That was nice of you. Especially since I don't think you *ever* go to the Healthy Eating Truck, ha!

HE: Okay, so maybe not, but it's nice to know it's there if I decide to **switch** from chocolate fudge to carrot sticks.

SHE: I probably shouldn't mention this, but . . .

HE: . . . but WHAT?

SHE: It's only 3:00. They're giving out the **Rookie** of the Year Award at 4:00 . . .

HE: Wait, WHAT?! So we didn't miss the whole festival? Let's get rolling! We can still make it!

SHE: Okay, I'm in. I'll head to the dairy aisle. I want to pick up some yogurt. Maybe we can save some time if you go find the cashier with the shortest line.

HE: Okay, good plan.

****** *a few minutes later* ******

SHE: Whoa! We only have 6 things. Why didn't you go to the Express Lane?

HE: I did. But today must be "Nobody Remembers How to Count Day" because *everyone* in the 10 Items Express Lane had a ton of things in their carts. This is the shortest line.

SHE: Okay, it may be the shortest line, and I think I know why . . . Do you see the big folder that woman is holding? Do you see how **thick** it is?

HE: Umm . . . Yes. What about it?

SHE: That folder is full of coupons. People who collect and organize coupons like that are called "extreme couponers." They save a ton of money, but it takes forever to **check out**! The cashier will ring up all her groceries, then the woman will take out all her millions and millions of coupons, then the cashier will scan each one of them. Did I mention there are millions and millions? Maybe BILLIONS of coupons! *Aaaarghhhh*!

HE: Okay, okay, I get it. She has a lot of coupons. Sheesh, I had no idea there's so much to learn about grocery shopping. Hey, look—quick! The self-checkout lane is empty . . . Let's get there FAST before somebody shows up!

SHE: Okay. But with all this **rushing around**, you owe me a caramel-fudge-whatever-it-was when we get to the festival.

HE: **It's a deal**!

YOUR TURN!

What do you remember from the previous sections? Write *True* or *False*. Answers are on page 230.

1. _____ All restaurants around campus will give students a discount.

2. _____ Your meal plan allows purchases only at campus cafés.

3. _____ Students with special food preferences can choose a different meal plan.

4. _____ A professional chef may be serving food on a truck.

5. _____ At a sit-down restaurant, you order your food at the counter, and then sit down.

6. _____ A tray of veggies is served as dessert.

7. _____ Chocolate chip cookies are delicious.

8. _____ You can cook soup and ramen noodles for a snack in your room.

9. _____ If someone demonstrates a product at the store, you can have a free taste.

10. _____ Most dining halls have a station where you can grab a slice of pizza and a soda.

BY THE WAY . . .

We're always forgetting things we need, so we make lots of quick trips to the grocery store to get the milk we forgot . . . or the bread . . . or the eggs . . . or the . . . well, you get the idea. We usually just need one or two things, and we're always in a hurry to get home, so we love the Express Lane. But can you guess what we *don't* love about the Express Lane? (Well, besides the people who have *100* items in the 10-item lane . . .) In most stores the signs say, "10 items or less!" and "20 items or less!" Are you wondering what's wrong with that? Or have you already figured it out? *Items* is a count noun! You can *count* the number of things in your cart! (Well, we're beginning to think some people can't count, haha.) We use *fewer* with count nouns, and *less* with non-count nouns. So those signs should read, "10 items or *fewer*!" and "20 items or *fewer*!"

Haha—never go shopping with an English teacher!

VOCABULARY

- **aisle:** place to walk in a store
- **appear:** show up unexpectedly
- **bag:** put groceries in a bag at the checkout counter
- **care package:** a box from home filled with lots of goodies!
- **cart:** the large basket with wheels that you push through the store as you shop
- **cereal:** dried flakes of grains; a typical breakfast. Many are sweetened.
- **chain restaurant:** one of a group of restaurants that are alike; often owned by the same company
- **check out:** (verb) what you do when you scan your groceries and pay for them (*You check out at the checkout counter!*)
- **checkout:** (noun) the place and process of checking something out (*You pay for your stuff at checkout.*)
- **checkout:** (adjective) descriptor for the counter where you pay and check out (*You pay at checkout, and you check out at the checkout counter.* HA! WE LOVE ENGLISH!!!)
- **cold cuts:** slices of cold cooked meats (such as ham or turkey)
- **come up with:** have a new idea about something
- **convenience:** something easy
- **convenience store:** a store that sells a little bit of everything, like hot coffee, freshly made food items, and some groceries. Convenient!
- **counter:** the table-like area for serving food in a fast food restaurant; the place where you check out at the grocery store
- **coupon:** a paper (or phone code) that gives you a discount on an item
- **crudités:** raw vegetables, often served with a creamy dip or sauce
- **cuisine:** food prepared in a special way
- ⓘ **it's a deal!:** I agree to that plan!
- **décor:** the decoration and furniture in a place
- ⓘ **deli:** short for delicatessen (which very few people say!); where you buy prepared foods and sliced meats and cheeses
- ⓘ **delish:** delicious! Yum!
- ⓘ **demo:** demonstration; display of food preparation or a product
- **demonstrator:** a person who shows how to prepare a food item, or who explains the product

- **department:** a section with one main job or product
- **dietary restriction:** a rule about what foods you can or cannot eat.
- **These can be religious rules, or health and personal preferences.**
- **dip:** a creamy sauce for chips or vegetables
- **ethnic:** having to do with a certain country or culture
- **express:** faster
- **Express Lane:** the fast lane in a grocery store . . . sometimes, HA.
- **extreme couponer:** person who collects and uses coupons to save money at the grocery store
- **factor:** an important thing to think about in making a decision
- **farmers' market:** a place where people who grow or make fresh stuff sell their stuff!
- **feature:** a quality or a part of something
- **fettuccine Alfredo:** a dish of pasta noodles with a sauce made of cheese and butter and cream. Oh, man, we want some NOW!!
- **floret:** the flowery part of the vegetable, without the stem
- ⓘ **foodie:** someone with a special interest in food and how it's prepared; a gourmet
- ⓘ **forget it!:** don't even think about that; give something no importance
- **grilled cheese:** a classic sandwich! Delicious cheese between two slices of bread and grilled in a pan with butter. Try it! (And invite us for lunch!)
- **grocery:** a store that sells groceries, which are food supplies!
- ⓘ **have/get your way:** do what you would prefer
- ⓘ **head to:** go to
- **health inspector:** official whose job is to check food suppliers for cleanliness
- **host:** person who plans activities for, and invites people to an event; also, the act of planning and inviting
- **icing:** the sweet creamy covering on a cake; also called frosting
- **impress:** surprise; make someone admire someone or something
- **in advance:** before the time
- **inexpensive:** affordable; at a low price
- **ingredients:** items needed to make a certain food dish
- **keep up with:** always know what's popular about something

- ⓘ **kidding:** joking; not serious
- • **lane:** aisle or passageway near a counter in a store
- • **line:** people standing and waiting for their turn
- • **lounge:** an area to relax
- • **mac and cheese:** macaroni with a cheese sauce. YUM!
- • **meal plan:** you pay for a certain amount of food in advance
- • **microwave:** the appliance that cooks your popcorn in 3 minutes!
- ⓘ **need a college degree:** a joking expression to say something is so complicated that you need advanced study to know how to do it.
- • **nickname:** an informal name for someone or something
- • **noodle:** a strip of pasta or dough
- ⓘ *(you're)* **on your own:** I don't want anything to do with that idea!
- ⓘ **packed:** really, really, REALLY crowded
- • **panic:** get extremely frightened or anxious
- • **park:** put a vehicle in a certain place to stay for a time
- • **passion:** love
- ⓘ **pick up:** buy
- ⓘ **picky eater:** someone who will eat only certain foods prepared in a certain way
- • **place an order:** tell the worker what you want
- ⓘ **pop up:** appear or show up suddenly
- • **prepared (foods):** already made
- ⓘ **pricey/pricier:** more expensive
- • **rain check:** a coupon that lets you buy an item at a sale price (given when the store runs out of the item)
- • **ramen:** quick-cooking noodles; usually in a soup
- • **rare:** lightly cooked so that the meat is red in the middle
- • **recipe:** the ingredients and directions for preparing a food item
- • **refund:** give money back
- • **regularly:** on a schedule
- ⓘ **rookie:** a newcomer; someone who is doing something for the first time
- ⓘ **rush around:** hurry; do many things in a very fast way
- • **salad:** a meal of fresh vegetables, often with lettuce or green leafy vegetables; other prepared foods served cold

- **sample:** an example (like a typical menu); also, a small portion of something to try
- **self-checkout:** scan your own groceries instead of having the cashier do it
- **shopping list:** a note of what you need from the store. (Ours is on our phone.)
- **sit-down restaurant:** where you relax and order your food from a server, who brings everything to your table
- ⓘ **skip:** ignore; omit (If you *skip* class, you don't show up. If you skip a meal, you don't eat that meal . . . something we never do, haha.)
- **slice:** one piece of pizza; also, a piece of bread, cake or pie; also, a thin cut piece of meat
- **snack tray:** a selection of snacks. YES!
- **splurge:** spend money freely, usually on something special
- **station:** an area of a dining hall serving one type of food
- **stick:** a vegetable cut into a long, thin piece, like a carrot *stick*, or a celery *stick*
- ⓘ **stock up on:** buy a lot of something to have when you need it
- ⓘ **straight from:** directly
- **sundae:** a fabulous ice cream treat with sweet sauce and whipped cream and fruit. YUM!
- **switch:** change
- **thick:** deep; very full
- **thin:** narrow, skinny, small
- **trend:** a style or popular idea or thing
- **unique:** different from anything else
- **use up:** finish all of something
- **vegan:** someone who does not eat or use *any* animal products
- **vegetarian:** someone who does not eat meat or some other animal products
- ⓘ **veggie:** vegetable
- ⓘ **what's in:** "What food is in the house for me to eat?"

USE YOUR WORDS!

Match the word or phrase to the best meaning or usage. Answers are on page 230.

a. it's a deal!

b. bag the groceries

c. foodie

d. packed

e. slice

f. unique

g. you need a college degree!

h. dip

i. deli

j. picky eater

1. _____ place to buy freshly prepared foods and sliced meats and cheeses

2. _____ This is very complicated to figure out!

3. _____ completely unlike anything else

4. _____ a creamy sauce for chips or vegetables

5. _____ Put the items in a bag at the register.

6. _____ Okay, I agree! Let's do it!

7. _____ someone who enjoys lots of fine, gourmet food

8. _____ too many people!

9. _____ someone who likes only certain foods

10. _____ one serving of pizza

There's a Lot to Do!

We got so excited thinking about all that food that we almost forgot . . . There's something else important about college, too: **registering** for classes. Classes are where you go between snacks . . . ha, *no no no no* . . . of course we're just kidding about that . . . ! (Or are we? Ha!) Registration is a really **hectic** time when students sign up for the classes they need and want for the semester. There are courses that the college requires *all* students to take. These are called, um . . . *required courses*. In fancy college language, they may be called **GER**s—General Education Requirements—or something similar. The required courses may be different at different colleges, but they are usually classes in writing, **humanities** and the **arts**, math, science, **physical education**, and foreign language. Many universities **exempt** international students from the foreign language requirement. In fact, students who have taken advanced courses in any subject before coming to college *may* be exempt from certain classes. The rules for this **vary**, so you MUST check with an advisor. Find out the rules at your school!

With all of these things to **consider**, first-year students sometimes think that registering for classes is a challenge. No worries! One common mistake that freshmen make is trying to take too many credits their first semester. Sure, you think, "I'll take 18 credits of GERs, then I can take all classes in my major." *No, don't do it*! That's too much! A typical **course load** is 15 credits, but a lot of colleges encourage freshmen to take just 12 for their first semester. A 12-credit schedule is the minimum to be considered a "full-time" student. And, of course, as an international student, you must take at least the minimum number of credits to stay in **status**. Remember—you need to keep those grades up! Don't take so many classes your first semester that you find it difficult to do your best work. If your **GPA** (grade point average) falls below a certain point, you will have a lot of explaining to do! You *do not* want to be on "**academic probation**." So 18 credits (that's SIX COURSES!) is just crazy! Ha, and now you know why freshmen must check with an advisor before registration!

Okay, so what are "credits" anyway? Most college courses are 3 or 4 *credit hours*. That just means how many hours the class meets each week in a semester. So, a 3-credit course will meet for a total of 3 hours in a week. Well, not exactly . . . A classroom "hour" is usually 50 minutes (we like that kind of math!). If you take a 3-credit course, you will usually meet for class 3 *hours* a week; this could mean 2 or 3 class meetings, depending on the course. And this is where good **strategy pays off**! If you plan your schedule right, you may have classes on 3 days a week, with 2 days off! Woo hoo! If your status allows, you may be able to work those 2 days . . . or have fun with more baseball games and shopping!

Here's an important thing to keep in mind: As an international student, you will probably have to take placement tests to determine the proper level for your classes, even if you have already taken English proficiency exams. It's possible, for example, that you may need to take remedial (sometimes called *developmental*) English or math classes before you can register for the classes you need for your degree. Usually these **remedial** classes must be completed before you can register for regular classes. Remedial credits *will not count* towards your major or graduation requirements. If you are a transfer student from another college, some of the credits you earned there will not be accepted by the new school. We know what you're thinking: "All that work for nothing!" Well, it *is* a **pain** that some courses won't transfer, but think of all you've learned in that class anyway! Or maybe you're thinking this: "Wow! I know all the stuff in this course already!" Good for you! Some colleges accept College Board CLEP (**C**ollege **L**evel **E**xamination **P**rogram) credits that may be earned by making a certain score on a content exam. However, this is another reason why you MUST meet with an advisor. Before you pay for this exam, find out if your college will accept the credits!

Probably the most common **snag** at registration is finding that a course you want is **closed**. That means the limit on the number of students in a class has been reached. Sorry—those kids got there before you! Look carefully at all the **sections** for the course. It may be that an 8:00 class is still available. HA! OF COURSE IT IS! Who wants to get up for an 8:00 class?! Not us! Freshmen sometimes are the last to register, and everyone needs the same classes, so the sections fill up quickly. But if you're completely **out of luck** with a class you need or want, don't panic. You can take it another **term**.

Remember too, that many courses have **prerequisites**. That means you cannot take the class until you've taken another course before it.

Once you have the required courses out of the way, you can decide on the courses you need and want for your major. A major is your main **area** of study—the subject area you want to **specialize** in. A major requires a certain total number of credit hours; some are required courses, and others you can choose. Once you decide on a major (usually after a year or two), you'll be assigned a new faculty advisor in the department. This advisor will help you choose specific courses for your interests, and **keep an eye on** your progress and grades. If you have lots of interests, it's possible to have a "double major"— where you meet the major credit requirements for two subjects. But students typically have a major and a **minor**: that is, a concentrated area of intensive study (the major) and a slightly less **intensive** concentration in another subject (the minor). Remember that you are not limited to courses in your major and minor. You can take as many electives as your schedule will allow (check with your advisor!). Electives can be in ANY subject you'd like to study . . . Dance class, anyone?

Okay, you figured it all out, you met with your advisor, you registered for the classes you want . . . now you just . . . **show up**! The first day of class is usually an introduction to the instructor and to the class material. The instructor will introduce herself, and she may ask the students to introduce themselves, too. She will give you information about the course and answer any questions you may have. Each student will get a copy of the course **syllabus**—this is important! The syllabus will have the instructor's **contact information** (email address, phone number, and her office location with the hours she will be there), as well as the expectations for the course. Read it carefully! It's important to note the instructor's policy on **absences** (WHAT?! Absences?! NO ABSENCES for you! There's too much to learn in every class session!), on grading, and on participating in class discussions. The syllabus will have a description of the course, a list of what materials you need (including books), and a statement of what the learning goals are. The syllabus will include an outline of the course assignments, along with the dates that each is due. The syllabus—it's a powerful little packet of paper!

THINK ABOUT IT

How was the registration process? Did you feel that you had enough information to choose your courses? Did you feel **frustrated** if you couldn't select a class that you really wanted? How comfortable were you with the resources available to help you? As a first-year student, you don't have to worry about choosing a major yet, but do you already know what field of study you're most interested in? Do you think it's possible for a freshman (or sophomore) in college to know what career they want to do for the rest of their lives?

BY THE WAY . . .

Oh no! Were you **closed out** of the course you really, really wanted to take? Or did you sign up for a course with your favorite professor, but see that there's a different instructor on the first day of class? Maybe you signed up for a class thinking it would be all about art history, but you find out the course is actually a **pottery** class. *Aaaarghhhh!* It's okay—you can **drop** it! Don't worry. It happens all the time! There's always a change period at the beginning of the semester when students can add, drop, or change a class with no penalty. And, because so many students are dropping and changing classes, there's a good chance that the one you really, really wanted will have a seat available now. **ADD** IT! The drop/add period is just for a short time though, so make the decision quickly. If you change a class after the drop/add time, you'll get a grade of **W** on your transcript. That means that you **withdrew** from the class. A "W" grade means no credit for the course! NOoooooo!!

LANGUAGE SPOT: PHRASAL VERBS—SEPARABLE AND INSEPARABLE

In Part 2 we looked at literal and idiomatic phrasal verbs. Did you think that's ALL there is to learn about these fun informal expressions? HA, sorry! There's plenty more to know about phrasals! (Of course there is . . . it's English!) So let's take a look now at *separable* and *inseparable* phrasal verbs.

SEPARABLE: You can *separate* the verb from the particle.

For example:

- **Turn on** something (start the power on something)

You can say:

- **Turn on** *the light*

And you can say:

- **Turn** *the light* **on**

The word *light* (as used here) is a noun. It can come *after* the phrasal verb, or *between* the verb and the particle. But it's different if you are using a pronoun. In that case, you *always* place the pronoun between the verb and particle. For example:

You can say:

- **Turn** *it* **on**

But you *can't* say:

- **Turn on** *it*

INSEPARABLE: You can *never* separate the verb from the particle whether it's a noun OR a pronoun.

For example:

- **Run into** someone (meet someone unexpectedly)

You can say

- I **ran into** *Andy* at the grocery store. I thought he was on vacation.

And you can say:

- I **ran into** *him* at the grocery store

But you *can't* say:

- I **ran** *Andy* **into** at the grocery store. I thought he was on vacation.

And you *can't* say:

- I **ran** *him* **into** at the grocery store.

Soooooo the big question is: How do you know if a phrasal verb is *separable* or *inseparable*? Well, you may know just because you have heard it used in a certain way. Or you can check a dictionary! Look for where the words *someone/somebody* or *something* are placed. (These words may be shown as *so/sb* or *sth*).

If you *can* separate the phrasal verb, *someone/so*, *somebody/sb* or *something/sth* will be written in the middle of the phrasal verb. If you *cannot* separate the phrasal verb, *someone/so*, *somebody/sb* or *something/sth* will be written after the particle.

> **Turn** *something/sth* **on** (separable)
> **Run into** *someone/so, somebody/sb* (inseparable)

Here are some common examples:

SEPARABLE

- **put away:** put something in its place
- **put off:** decide to do something later instead of now
- **put up:** give someone a place to stay for a time
- **put up:** build something/put something on the wall
- **wake up:** stop sleeping!
- **mess up:** make something not perfect

INSEPARABLE

- **get away:** go someplace different
- **get by:** go past an obstacle
- **get around:** avoid something; also, way to go someplace
- **sign up:** place your name to join something
- **ease up:** become less strict

TRY IT!

Fill in the blanks with a phrasal verb from the group above. Answers are on page 231.

1. After exams, I just want to _____ from campus and relax.

2. The only reason I don't cook is that I don't want to _____ the kitchen.

3. I want to _____ the groceries before I eat all the snacks!

4. The instructor assigned three projects the first week of class! I hope she plans to _____ a little.

5. We have to _____ early for the trip to Washington.

6. I can _____ my sister _____ in the dorm, but not her pooch!

7. The professor _____ the test _____ until next week. Yay!

8. We like to _____ campus on our bikes.

9. Workers are fixing the road, but cars can _____ them.

10. If I don't _____ the cookies _____ now, I'll finish them all!

DIALOGUE: AUDIO TRACK 9

Herpetology?!

SHE: Man, I'm exhausted! I **had no idea** registration would be so stressful! I think I need to take a nap!

HE: Huh? I just registered online, and it only took me about 20 minutes! What problem did you have? Didn't you have all the courses planned out with your advisor?

SHE: Well, yeah, I did, but the music elective I wanted to take was closed, so I had to come up with a Plan B. Then my Plan B art class was also closed, so I had to come up with *another* elective that I really don't think I want to take . . . in **herpetology**! I'm not sure how much I need to learn about turtles.

HE: Haha! Oh come on, everyone likes turtles . . . that could **turn out** to be your favorite class!

SHE: Well, I'm not so sure about that, but I'm keeping this schedule for now. But if a new section of art or music opens up, I plan to drop herpetology and add the art. Anyway, this keeps me at 12 credit hours, so I won't mess up my GPA. I plan to graduate with honors!

HE: Well, can you put off the electives until next year, and just take another course in your major?

SHE: I haven't **declared** a major yet, but it will probably be economics. And I've actually been thinking about a double major, economics with art or music. So you can see that herpetology isn't really on my list.

HE: Yes, and I can also see why trying to figure all that out makes you want to take a nap! I'll text you later. Maybe when you wake up another section of Intro to Art will be open.

SHE: Yeah, a nap is one way to get around worrying about my schedule. But if I start dreaming about turtles, I'll know I'm in trouble!

YOUR TURN!

What do you remember from the previous sections? Write *True* **or** *False*. **Answers are on page 231.**

1. _____ Once you enroll in classes, you can't change your schedule.

2. _____ You need to declare a major immediately and take only those classes.

3. _____ Everyone must take the same general education requirements.

4. _____ If a course section is closed, you can't register for the course.

5. _____ If you need to take a remedial class, those credits probably will not count towards your graduation total.

6. _____ You must take a minimum of 12 credit hours to stay legally as a student in the United States.

7. _____ Credits in a foreign language course are required.

8. _____ The course syllabus is a summary of what will be covered in the class, as well as due dates for projects, and what rules the professor has established for the class.

9. _____ If you transfer from one college to another, your course credits will also transfer.

10. _____ A minor can be in any area of interest . . . even if it's not related to the major.

BY THE WAY . . .

So . . . are you taking a *course*? Are you taking a *class*? Are you following a *program of studies*? Yes. Yes. And yes!

- *Course* usually refers to the name of the subject you are studying for the semester.

  "This *course* is Economics 101."

- *Class* can also refer to the subject.

  "I'm taking an economics *class* this semester." (He registered for an economics *course*.)

- *Class* also refers to a single meeting.

  "I can't have another cup of coffee—I'm late for *class*!" (Today's lesson starts very soon!)

- And just to keep things tricky, we commonly use *course* and *class* to mean the same thing.

  "Welcome! We'll start *class* in just a minute. But first, this is Economics 101. If it's not the *class* you registered for, you're in the wrong place." (He'll start the day's lesson after he's sure everyone registered for the right course!)

Here's the easy part: One specific session is always a *class*. If you're talking about the instruction you're getting right now, in this seat, with the professor explaining a theory right now, then you're talking about *this class*. Just this one *class*, today, right here, right now. Haha, or maybe you're talking about the *class* YOU'RE GOING TO BE LATE FOR, if you don't hurry up and get out of bed!!

- *Program of Studies* usually refers to the major area of study that you choose, and all the courses that you take to complete the program. American students usually say *major* to talk about their programs of study.

VOCABULARY

- **absence:** missing a class; not being present for a class
- **academic probation:** in danger of failing because of poor grades— this can affect your enrollment status in school! DO NOT experience academic probation!
- **add:** enroll in another class; add a class to your schedule

- **area:** field, range
- **arts:** music, dance, art, and areas that add to quality of life
- **closed out:** not able to register for a class because it's full
- **closed:** class has no space for more students; class is full
- **consider:** think about carefully
- **contact information:** the ways to communicate with your teacher (usually office phone, email address, and office location and hours)
- **course load:** the total number of credits (classes) you are taking
- **credit hours:** the number of hours the class meets per week
- **declare:** formally decide on
- **drop:** remove a course from your schedule
- **exempt:** you don't have to follow the rule!
- **frustrated:** feeling annoyed because you can't be successful at doing something
- **GER:** General Education Requirements
- **GPA:** Grade Point Average
- ⓘ **have no idea:** not know about something
- **hectic:** very busy, usually doing many things
- **herpetology:** study of reptiles and amphibians. TURTLES!
- **humanities:** study of literature, art, philosophy, history, religion, and other human experience
- **intensive:** demanding; concentrating on the topic
- ⓘ **keep an eye on:** watch carefully
- **minor:** area of interest or study; less intensive than the major
- ⓘ **out of luck:** too bad! not able to do something you want to do
- ⓘ **a pain:** something annoying
- ⓘ **pay off:** have a reward, or good, happy result
- **physical education** (also known as *PE* or *gym*): a class focused on keeping the body active and healthy
- **pottery:** ceramics, objects made from clay, or making these objects
- **prerequisite:** needed before something else
- **register:** enroll, sign up
- **remedial:** providing help to improve skills in an area
- **section:** part
- ⓘ **show up:** attend; go to a place

- ⓘ **snag:** problem
- **specialize:** focus on one subject to know a lot
- **status:** your legal (or visa) situation
- **strategy:** plan
- **syllabus:** paper explaining the course and requirements
- **term:** semester; the length of time in school to complete a course
- ⓘ **turn out:** become; be the result
- **vary:** change
- ⓘ **W:** withdraw
- **withdraw** (withdrew): drop out of a course after the change deadline, with no credit

USE YOUR WORDS!

Complete the sentences below with a new word or phrase from the previous sections. Try to do it without looking at the vocabulary list. Hey, we'll even help you by giving you the first letter! (You're welcome. ☺) Answers are on page 232.

1. The first week of school is so **h**_____ ! I feel like I need to do a million things at one time.

2. It was a perfect plan for fun in the city! The only **s**_____ was finding a way to get there.

3. At the meeting he talked with another person working on a documentary. They exchanged **c**_____ and will try to meet so they can work together.

4. She really wanted a class with that very popular teacher, but so did everyone else! She was **o**_____; the class was closed 20 minutes after registration started!

5. She's hoping some people won't **s**_____ on the first day of class. Then she'll try again to register.

6. Haha—Everyone thought this course would be a piece of cake, but it **t**_____ to be the hardest class of the semester!

7. I love spending the day in the city, but taking the crowded train during the morning commute can really be a **p**_____.

8. The rules **v**_____ about how many electives you can take. Check with your advisor.

9. It may seem like hard work now, but it will really **p**_____ when you get that FABULOUS job after graduation!

10. Will you **k**_____ my bag for a minute? I need to go outside to make a quick phone call.

MORE HELP IS ON THE WAY!

We know what you're thinking. You're thinking, "Registration was the easy part. I've got courses and textbooks and projects and assignments and homework and papers . . . *aaack*! Now what?" Here's what: YOU'LL BE FINE! You did the most difficult part already— you worked hard, you managed all the rules and procedures for getting here, and YOU'RE HERE! We think you won't have any problems . . . BUT . . . just in case . . . there are plenty of people, programs, and processes to help you if you need a little extra support with your classwork. Of course, you're new to the expectations of American professors, and you may be feeling just a bit unsure about what to do. Remember—your professor will be happy to help. Check those office hours! You may feel more comfortable just talking to the instructor about the assignment. But if you still need some help doing the work—NO WORRIES!

WRITING CENTER

Maybe you feel that you just need a little extra help as you write your papers. Maybe you're not sure how to start an assignment . . . or what information will best support your ideas. Many professors require that papers be written according to very strict guidelines, and you may not be familiar with that **style**. Your college has just the help you need!

The Writing Center is a place designed for exactly one purpose—to help students organize their ideas and express them in a clear and correct way. You can get help in the **format** of a paper for your class, and the style (and **font**!) that your professor prefers. Someone can help you with using **citations** and **references** to support your ideas. Are you comfortable with writing a **thesis**? If not, the Writing Center staff can help you form your ideas into a statement for your paper. How can you support your important points? What type of **evidence** from professional sources will support your ideas? As an international student, you may simply want someone to help you with grammar. (Haha, we know the pain of that past perfect progressive!) Grammar, style, usage, citations . . . The Writing Center staff is there to help you figure it all out. Together, you and the staff can analyze and improve your writing. And, do we need to say it? . . . It's just for you! And it's FREE! Go on—they're waiting for you!

TUTORING CENTER

Okay, your writing is great—lucky you! Maybe you'd just like to review some difficult material before a big exam. Maybe there's a really tough assignment that you're worried about. Everyone needs a little help sometimes. Well, if you got lucky, maybe your roommate is an astrophysics and math genius! She can probably help you with your *Discrete Probability and Differential Equation Theory of Statistical Combinatorics and Vector Variable Analysis* assignment! Lucky you! (Hmm . . . or you can ask us. We will have no idea what you're talking about, but you can ask. haha.) Or you can go to the Tutoring Center. Sometimes the Center will have people available to help anytime you want to go in. Sometimes you may make an appointment for a certain time. If you're having difficulty with any subject, the Center will match you up with someone who can help you understand the material. You and the tutor will come up with a schedule that's convenient for both of you. Do you need to meet just once to help understand one problem? **Easy peasy**! Do you need to meet once a week until you feel that you're able to understand the material on your own? You and the tutor will figure out what time is best. Together you'll come up with a plan. Yay! **Ace** that course!

ESL TUTORS AND CONVERSATION PARTNERS

Yes! Tutoring just for *you*! Writing? Speaking? Listening? Reading? Yes, yes, yes, and YES! The ESL department will have all kinds of resources to help you with your English. ESL tutors are specially trained to help international students with their specific issues. It's a really good idea to see the same tutor each time so you can establish a good working relationship and they can get to know you and your English skills. There may be after-class discussion groups, just so you can practice your English. These groups often discuss cultural issues, like . . . hmm . . . the "problem" of American food, ha! ESL tutors can help with all kinds of cultural questions you may have. There will be plenty of study groups where students get together in an informal group to practice speaking and to discuss problems with classwork. Many colleges have programs to match an international student with a native English speaker, for speaking practice and to see cultural differences and similarities **one-on-one**. Lots of times the student and their partner will visit interesting places together, or go to a local restaurant. It's great practice, and it's fun! And, of course, there are plenty of academic English resources to help you with grammar and other English language topics.

ADVISORS

You know . . . YOU. You know what your goals are, and what you'd like to do at college. That's fabulous! But sometimes it can be tricky figuring out exactly how to get there. What's the best way to **accomplish** your goals— academic and personal? How can you get to where you *want* to be as you manage this new American culture, experience, and lifestyle? The good news is that you've done the hard part already—you've figured out what you want. (Hmm—but no worries if you haven't quite got there yet—advisors can help you figure that out too!) Your academic advisor is more than just a source for course information. Your advisor can **sit down with** you and take a look at your schedule . . . and talk about your goals. Advisors have plenty of experience helping students manage their time. They can offer suggestions on how to stay focused on your academics while you still enjoy a healthy (and fun!) personal life. Sure, you *should* take fun trips to nearby (or faraway!) cities! You *should* go to baseball games and cool concerts! You *should* volunteer with your club for community events! You *should* attend as many campus events as you can! It's all about time management and **balance**, and your academic advisor is a genius at helping figure out balance, ha! There really is time for everything—if you plan it right. Your academic advisor can help with that plan.

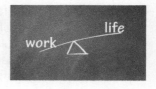

Okay, so now that you've got a time management plan . . . what's next? Think about it—with the differences in teaching and academic styles between your country and your new university, are you comfortable with the best ways to study? Are you comfortable with taking notes in class? Are you comfortable with ways to learn and use new vocabulary? Are you comfortable figuring out how to **highlight** the most important ideas in a teacher's lesson? We call these *study skills*, and they'll help you make the best use of your study time. Your academic advisor can give you some great tips on what to study and *how* to study! Your advisor will have ideas on how to work with a study group, how to take notes in class, how to summarize a lesson, and how to practice what you've learned. Wow—those advisors are like geniuses! They know everything, haha!

You're probably thinking that academic advisors must be the most popular people on campus. Well, that's why they have **scheduled** office hours! Make sure you know *where* the office is, and *when* the advisor can meet with you. And don't forget—your instructor also *wants* to help you be successful—so meet with her during her office hours too! FIND THOSE OFFICES! CHECK THOSE HOURS! TALK TO THOSE PEOPLE!

Oh, and by the way . . . don't forget another really good resource for help: your RA. The RA (Resident Advisor) in your dorm is a student (just like you!) who is specially trained to have lots of answers to questions, and lots of solutions to problems. Just ask!

THINK ABOUT IT

Many American colleges think it's very important for students to have a good *liberal arts* education. This means that in addition to your major course of study you must take courses to learn *something* about *everything*: the arts, math and the sciences, culture, society, literature, world languages . . . Do you think a liberal arts education helps students become better citizens of the world? Is it important for everyone to study different subjects outside of their main interest? Or do you think students should be required to take courses only in their major field of study, and concentrate on that? How important is it to have a broad education, covering many topics?

BY THE WAY . . .

 You may be able to register for some online or **hybrid** courses in your subject. A course that is fully online means that there are no face-to-face classroom meetings. All the work is completed online, and discussions take place in online forums. A **hybrid** course has much of the material presented online, with most of the assignments and discussion online, but there is also some classroom meeting time. It's the **best of both worlds!**

However, be careful with online courses outside of what your department or university offers. Some online schools may offer courses that sound great . . . until you find out that your university won't accept them. Many online schools are not **accredited**, and the courses you pay for will not be recognized by colleges OR by future employers! In fact, some **for-profit** online universities have been **investigated** by the government for **fraud**—falsely promising students a degree or a good job. Some of these "colleges" have taken students' money, and then the school has **gone out of business**. If the students took out **loans** to pay for the school, they are still required to pay back the loans. And some "online courses" are just **scams** to get your **personal information** . . . and your money! Be careful. Check with your department or advisor before you take online courses that are not offered by your school. Do your homework!

LANGUAGE SPOT: COMMON EXPRESSIONS

Have we mentioned peanut butter and jelly? A million times? Peanut butter and jelly just go together (and we'll show you how in just a minute!). Here are some other really common expressions in English that just go together . . . you know, like peanut butter and jelly. (Haha, but you can't eat these!)

- **ins and outs:** all the details and facts about how something works
- **dos and don'ts:** the rules! what you can and can't do!
- **odds and ends:** different items, details, or little jobs you need to do
- **pros and cons:** the reasons for and against something

- **ups and downs:** good times and bad times

- **to and fro:** back and forth! To one place and back again

- **back and forth:** to and fro! A movement backward and forward, or side to side; also a conversation or disagreement

- **over and out:** "That's it. I'm finished. I have nothing more to say."

- **comes and goes:** happens sometimes, for a short time, then it goes away or stops

- **off and on:** now and then; sometimes

- **rise and shine:** Wake up and get started!

- **up and running:** set up, fixed, and in working order! "Finally, the new computer system is up and running!"

TRY IT!

Choose which expression fits the situations below. Answers are on page 232.

1. His hand doesn't hurt all the time. The pain _____.

2. She was texting her friend when the professor entered class. She texted good-bye by saying _____ ; then she put away her phone.

3. It wasn't a perfect day for baseball. It was raining _____ all day.

4. It didn't take long for the new student to learn all the _____ of living in a dorm.

5. After considering the _____ of a double major, she decided to concentrate on just one area of study.

6. Living with a roommate has _____ . Sometimes it's a fabulous fun experience, and sometimes it's tricky.

7. The debate about the new policy went _____ , with each side explaining their reasons.

8. He was so nervous about meeting the president that he kept walking _____ across the waiting room.

9. Her dad woke her every morning by knocking on the door and saying in a funny voice, "_____!"

10. Everything was packed for the trip, except for a few _____ they decided to keep in the car with them.

DIALOGUE: AUDIO TRACK 10

A Little Extra Help

TUTOR: Hello again, it's good to see you. What would you like to work on today?

STUDENT: Last week we worked on the overall **structure** of my essay for my history class. I think that's in pretty **good shape**, so could you just **proofread** it for grammar errors today, please?

TUTOR: Well, we can definitely take a look at your grammar and work on it together. That was your essay about early European settlers in America, wasn't it? Why don't you read the first section to me and let's see what we can find.

******** *(student reads)* ********

TUTOR: Okay, I see that you have a couple of errors with word form.

STUDENT: What do you mean by that?

TUTOR: It means that, for example, maybe you are using a verb instead of an adjective. Can you find any words that might be incorrect?

STUDENT: Oh yes. Here I write *prosper cities*, but it should it be *prosperous*.

TUTOR: Yes, that's exactly right. Great! Here's another one: *the evolve* of society. What should that be?

STUDENT: Um . . . is it *evolved*?

TUTOR: Try again.

STUDENT: I know! *Evolution*.

TUTOR: Exactly right! Also remember you are writing about the past so you need to be using the past tense. You have a lot correct, but one or two are wrong. Look at this section . . .

STUDENT: Ah yes, it should be *spoke* instead of *speak*, and *provided* instead of *provide*.

TUTOR: Yes, and here you have *leaded* as the past of *lead*, but that's an irregular verb.

STUDENT: *Led*, right?

TUTOR: Yep! Another thing I can see, and it's not wrong exactly . . . you use the word *said* a lot. In this paragraph you have the word *said* 5 times. There are lots of words you can use instead of *said* that are much stronger. If you use a thesaurus you can get lots of words with the same or similar meaning. When you go through this again, highlight all the times you use the word *said* and try to vary it.

STUDENT: Okay, good idea.

TUTOR: Now I understand what you are trying to say here but it sounds a little **awkward**. You wrote, "Many people felt lonely and were hard to adapt to the new environment." Can you think of a better way to say that?

STUDENT: Hmmmmmm . . . was *hard*?

TUTOR: Almost . . .

STUDENT: *was hard adapting*?

TUTOR: Okay, you're almost there. Maybe something like this: "Many people felt lonely, and it was hard for them to adapt to the new environment." How does that sound?

STUDENT: Sounds good! Let me write that down before I forget.

TUTOR: Okay, I also see you have several errors with **articles**.

STUDENT: Yes, we don't use them in Korean so they're really hard for me.

TUTOR: Yes, articles and **prepositions** are such small words, but they are some of the most difficult words to get right. Let's take a look at the next section and focus on those . . .

YOUR TURN!

What do you remember from the previous sections? Write *True* or *False*. Answers are on page 232.

1. _____ Your professor will arrange a time for you to go to the Writing Center.

2. _____ An ESL tutor will help with cultural questions as well as academic ones.

3. _____ A liberal arts college provides only fine arts programs.

4. _____ Hybrids save money on gas.

5. _____ Schools or employers may not accept some courses you may see online.

6. _____ The RA (Resident Advisor) in your dorm is a faculty member who is there to advise you.

7. _____ The Tutoring Center is only for students who are failing a course.

8. _____ A *scam* is an online course that is not in your major.

9. _____ The smaller the word, the easier it is to learn.

10. _____ Tutors will write your paper with you.

BY THE WAY . . .

Registration? Done! Yay. Let's celebrate! This is a perfect occasion for a nice relaxing dinner at the sit-down restaurant off-campus. When you go, the person greeting you may ask if you prefer a table or a **booth**. Table: You know this one—the chairs are arranged around a table. That's easy! For large **parties**, a few tables may be placed together. A *booth* is a table with two comfortable benches facing each other. The **benches** are often cushioned, with high backs, and two or three people can sit next to each other. We like booths—somehow they seem cozier and more comfortable. Some casual restaurants even have space at a counter where people can eat. Wherever you sit, enjoy your dinner! You deserve it after a crazy day of figuring out registration!

VOCABULARY

- **accomplish:** achieve; complete something
- **accredited:** officially recognized; meeting standards and requirements for an organization or school
- ⓘ **ace:** get an A grade! Perfect score!
- **articles:** a, an, the
- **awkward:** not correct; odd; uncomfortable
- ⓘ **balance:** giving importance to all parts
- **bench:** a long seat for several people
- ⓘ **best of both worlds:** having the advantages (and best parts) of two systems
- **booth:** a partly enclosed seating area in a restaurant

- **citation:** a quote from another source
- ⓘ **easy peasy:** Wow—it's so easy!
- **evidence:** proof; information from a source that supports an idea
- **font:** the size and style of print
- **for-profit:** in business to make money
- **format:** the way a page looks, or the way a paper is written
- **fraud:** lying about something in order to get money; this is against the law—a crime!
- **go out of business:** stop doing business, often because the business has not been successful, or the owner has moved
- ⓘ **in good shape:** in good condition
- **highlight:** make a note of the importance of something
- **hybrid:** using different systems (a car using gas *and* an electric battery; a course that is taught online *and* in the classroom)
- **investigate:** examine facts about something, especially if there may be a problem or a crime!
- **liberal arts:** a combination of non-technical subjects, such as arts and humanities
- **loan:** money that is borrowed from a bank (or a person) for a time, then paid back later
- **one-on-one:** one person helping one other person; face-to-face
- **party:** oh, you know about the fun one, ha, but it also means the group at a restaurant or event
- **personal information:** facts about you, which may include bank account numbers. DO NOT GIVE OUT THIS INFORMATION, except to trusted people, face-to-face—never online!
- **prepositions:** small words introducing phrases, like, *on* the desk, *in* the room, *at* the dorm
- **proofread:** read something carefully to look for and correct mistakes
- **reference:** information from a source that supports an idea
- **scam:** a trick; an illegal plan to get information or money
- **scheduled:** planned for certain times
- **should:** we strongly advise you to do it
- **sit down with someone:** spend time with someone to discuss something
- **structure:** organization
- **style:** the way something is presented or written
- **thesis:** in a paper, the statement of the idea you want to prove

USE YOUR WORDS!

Complete the sentences with a new word or phrase from the previous section. Choose from the words below. Answers are on page 233.

ace	highlight
loan	party
scam	hybrid
format	accomplish
easy peasy	in good shape

1. The restaurant table was only big enough for a _____ of four.

2. Her advisor told her the online school was a _____. There were no classes, and no college or company would accept the "degree."

3. He studied so hard for the test! He was sure he would _____ it.

4. My grandma always said "If you really work hard, you can _____ anything!"

5. I thought a PE class would be _____, but it's hard work getting up at 8 A.M. to go running.

6. I'm taking a _____ course this semester. It's nice to meet up with the others once a week, but it's also great to do assignments online in my **PJs**.

7. I like to _____ important sentences as I read. Then later I can find them easily to use as quotations.

8. The worst part about graduating and getting a job is having to use some of the paycheck to pay back your student _____.

9. I thought I just had to write a paper! I didn't know it had to be in a special _____ with a 12-point font!

10. Okay, I've checked my paper three times now and corrected everything I can. I think it's _____ to give to my professor.

FUN WITH IDIOMATIC EXPRESSIONS: School

- **class act:** someone who always does things in a very kind or polite way; very stylish
  *Rox is a **class act**! She's a great example of how to behave well, even in a bad situation.*

- **hit the books:** begin to study really hard
  *I have a big test Friday. I plan to **hit the books** all week!*

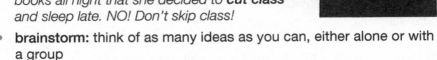

- **cut class/skip class:** Nooo! Don't do it! It means you do not attend a scheduled class.
  *Our crazy friend was so tired from hitting the books all night that she decided to **cut class** and sleep late. NO! Don't skip class!*

- **brainstorm:** think of as many ideas as you can, either alone or with a group
  *The video production team **brainstormed** ideas about how to film when the cafeteria was empty.*

- **A for effort:** Well, maybe it wasn't a perfect result, but you tried really hard.
  *The ice in his science project melted before he explained the purpose. Oh well, **A for effort**!*

- **show of hands:** a way to vote; raise your hand if you like the idea
  *When he suggested a place for the after-season party, the team captain asked for a **show of hands** to vote on it.*

- **draw a blank:** be unable to think of an answer, even if you studied
  *I know this, I know this, I know this, I know this . . . aaack! But I'm **drawing a blank** now!*

- **take attendance/roll:** make a note of who is present or absent from class or a meeting
  *Hey, sorry I'm late. Did the teacher already **take attendance**?*

- **goof off:** play around instead of working at something; not take something seriously
  *My crazy roommate decided to **goof off** instead of finishing her project.*

- **out to lunch:** confused; not paying attention to what's going on; a little crazy/silly
  *I asked about the test and she started talking about the bus schedule. She's a little **out to lunch** today.*

but also literally:

- **out to lunch:** gone from a place to have lunch
  *I went to the instructor's office, but she was **out to lunch**. I'll go back in an hour.*

TRY IT!

Match the situation with the idiom. Answers are on page 233.

a. draw a blank   d. skip/cut class
b. hit the books   e. brainstorm
c. show of hands

1. _____ Do NOT do this if you want a good grade!

2. _____ You studied last night, but you're a little nervous, so you may do this when the professor asks a question.

3. _____ Everyone thinks of lots of ideas at the same time.

4. _____ Uh-oh. Trouble on the last test? This is what you need to do.

5. _____ The instructor asks the class to vote: project due *before*, or *after*, spring break?

JUST FOR FUN!

Come on, you know you want to try one! It's a classic! You can ask just about anyone if they've had a PB&J, and they will say "Of course!" Eating peanut butter and jelly sandwiches for lunch is a part of growing up for most American kids. We think it's the all-American sandwich. It's easy! It's delicious! And it even has its own, ahem, *SIMILE*: "They're a perfect couple! They go together *like peanut butter and jelly*." That means that two things (or people!) make a perfect match . . . they are a perfect pair. Okay, did we make you hungry? Let's get started . . .

A Perfect PB&J

Ingredients:

- A jar of peanut butter (creamy or **crunchy**)
- A jar of grape jelly (that's the classic flavor)
- Two slices of bread
- A knife for **spreading**
- A plate

Directions:

- Put a slice of bread on the plate.
- With a knife, **scoop** some peanut butter from the jar onto the bread, and spread it.
- Do the same with the jelly.
- Put the second slice of bread on top.
- Cut the sandwich in half.
- Hurry! Eat it quickly before someone else wants it!

TIP: Bottomless Beverages!

Are you thirsty? You're in luck! Most restaurants in the U.S. offer **"bottomless" beverages** when you order a meal. What is *bottomless*? Well, it means you will never see the *bottom* of the glass. Okay, that may not be exactly true, but what it means is that your server will **refill** your coffee, or tea, or soda at no extra charge. **Unlimited** refills! *Free* refills! You may even see it on the menu, or on a sign in the restaurant: FREE REFILLS! Most times, you don't even have to ask for a refill—the waiter will simply see that your glass is not full, and POOF!—like magic, a new, full glass of soda is on the table for you!

But what if you're at a fast food restaurant? No waiters. No worries! The same free-refill policy applies. At a fast food restaurant you may get a cup when you pay for your meal at the counter. You bring the cup to the soda machine, and you can fill it yourself. And again . . . and again . . . and again . . . and . . . *urp*.

This applies to drinks like soda and coffee, but it does NOT apply to *all* beverages. For example, drinks that come in a bottle or a can are *not* replaced for free. Drinks like milk or juice or fruit beverages are not refilled. You will be charged for each glass (or order) of those drinks.

TIP: Doggie Bags . . . (but not at the buffet)

Do you know about *doggie bags*? You may know that a doggie is a little pooch . . . and a bag is . . . well, a *bag*. When you put them together, you get one of the cool parts about eating out in a restaurant! Maybe you've noticed that **serving** sizes in American restaurants are pretty big. You get a LOT of food! If you're like us, it's too much food to finish at one meal. That's where the doggie bag comes in! When you've finished your meal, your server usually asks, "Can I take that for you?" That means they want to take away dishes that you've finished. But if there is food left on the plate, the server may ask, "Can I wrap that for you?" or "Do you want a *to go* box?" If he doesn't ask, you can say, "I'd like a doggie bag, please" or "Will you wrap that, please?"

Can you guess why it's called a *doggie bag*? Haha, some people don't want to admit that they like to eat **leftovers**—so they pretend the extra food is for their . . . *doggie*! Not us! We're happy to admit that we'll eat that **yummy** food tomorrow! Those leftovers will make another delicious restaurant meal—without the restaurant! And without . . . THE COOKING! YAY!

There is one type of restaurant where you can't get a doggie bag, however. (And it's one of our favorites!) At a ***buffet*** (we pronounce it *buff-ay*) restaurant you pay one price, then choose from many, many, many, *many* (you get the idea) different food items. The food items are in very large serving bowls or pans, and you can take as much food as you like. If you want **seconds** (Wow! You must be really hungry!), you can go back to the serving station as many times as you want! But you can forget about a doggie bag here. At a buffet, you can have as much food as you like, but you must eat it in the restaurant. You can't take any food home. (I think you can see why! If we were allowed to take doggie bags from a buffet, we'd bring our suitcase to the restaurant, haha!)

This is not a doggie bag!

 ROAD TRIP: It's a Dude Ranch, Dude!

Have you ever seen an American **cowboy** movie? You know the ones we're talking about: Cowboys with big hats ride big horses on big **ranches**. **Herds** of cattle **roam** freely. Beautiful **snow-capped** mountains rise up **in the distance**. The American West! Ranching—**raising cattle**, horses and sheep—is a main **occupation** in the West, and you can experience it for yourself. Yes, we're talking about ***Dude Ranching***. Lots of places in the West have dude ranches just for tourists. Yes, a dude ranch, dudes! You can be a cowboy (or cowgirl) for a week! Cool!

There are tons of cool things to do if you stay at a dude ranch. You can go horseback riding on the ranch, go fishing in **streams** or rivers, go swimming in local "**swimmin' holes**," and go **whitewater rafting** down wild rivers. Sleep at the ranch, or camp outside under the stars. Sing songs and tell stories around a campfire, with only the moon and the fire to light the night. Best of all—wear your cool cowboy hat EVERYWHERE!

If this sounds like the American road trip of your dreams, you're in luck. Consider what you'd like to do, then do your homework. There are lots of different types of dude ranches. You may want to choose a "working" ranch. On a *working* dude ranch you get to do all the cowboy **chores** yourself. Maybe you'll cook meals over a campfire. Maybe you'll **shear** sheep. Maybe you'll herd

horses into a **corral**. **Count us out** for this dude ranch—we have a hard enough time corralling our little pooches into the backyard!

But wait! There's another type of ranch too! It's a **RESORT** dude ranch. These ranches are designed for luxury. There are plenty of fun outdoor activities, but instead of staying in a simple **cabin** (or **tent**!), you can choose a fancy room . . . with beautiful **views** of the mountains . . . and comfortable furniture . . . and wifi . . . and gourmet meals! Hmm . . . Sign us up for that one! Let's go, dudes!

✅ QUICK FACTS

✓ We think of these states as "the West": Idaho, Montana, Wyoming, Nevada, Colorado, and Utah; but different sources may include other states and regions.

✓ After Columbus's voyage, many European explorers came to North America and **claimed** the land for their countries. (Of course, the land was already settled by the Native Americans who lived there, but that's another story!) Around the 1800s, the new United States of America began to **acquire** western lands, and in the 1840s, people from the east began moving to this new **territory**. They were looking to get rich by **gold mining**. This was called "The Gold Rush."

✓ This *Gold Rush* time in U.S. history is what we usually think of when we watch **Westerns**. Westerns are movies about the old-time West, with cowboys, train robberies, and horse chases; about newly settled towns with "good guys" and "bad guys" and very few laws. It was the Wild Wild West!

ANY QUESTIONS?

Are you wondering if there are still cowboys (and cowgirls!) today? The land in the West is very good for **grazing** cattle and raising sheep, and that's where much of our beef comes from. (Remember that steak in your doggie bag? Maybe it came from a ranch in Montana!) The job is still the same: taking care of the animals, but we often just call these modern cowboys *ranchers*.

Are there cowboys/cowgirls/ranchers in big cities? Ha— well, yes and no! Of course there are no ranches, and no cattle or sheep roam freely in the big cities. (That would be pretty funny to see, wouldn't it?) But there are plenty of people who like to wear cowboy hats and cowboy boots. In fact, Texas is kind of famous for its cowboy boots and hats. Wild!

VOCABULARY

- **acquire:** get; obtain for yourself to own
- **beverage:** a drink
- **bottomless:** there's no bottom!
- **buffet:** a table or serving station with lots of food choices (for one price); You can eat as much as you want.
- **cabin:** a small, very basic house made of wood
- **cattle:** cows
- **chores:** little jobs that are your responsibility to do
- **claim:** say that something belongs to you
- **corral:** v: gather animals into a fenced area; n: the fenced area for animals to stay
- ⓘ **count** (someone) **out:** Don't include me!
- **cowboy/cowgirl:** person who rides horses and works on a ranch
- **crunchy:** has small bits of nuts
- ⓘ **dude:** pal! friend! guy! (slang!)
- **dude ranch:** a vacation place where people can do ranch and outdoor activities.
- **gold mining:** looking for gold in rivers and rocks
- **graze:** move in a slow and relaxed way, eating grass (or whatever cows eat, ha!)

- **herd:** n: a large group of animals; v: gather animals into a group
- **in the distance:** far away, but able to be seen
- **leftovers:** extra food from a meal
- **occupation:** job
- ⓘ **PJs:** pajamas; the comfy clothes you wear to bed
- **rafting:** floating down a river in a sturdy canvas or rubber boat-like structure
- **raise:** grow; take care of something until it's grown
- **ranch:** a place where the jobs are taking care of horses, cows, and sheep
- **refill:** another serving of a drink. Thank you!
- **resort:** a fancy place to go for vacation
- **roam:** move about from place to place
- **scoop:** get or gather something with a spoon or a similar utensil
- **seconds:** having another serving of food after you've finished the first!
- **serving:** the amount of food for one person at a meal
- **shear:** give a sheep a haircut; cut the wooly hair from sheep
- **snow-capped:** snow at the very top
- **spread:** using a tool (or knife), move a substance over the surface of something
- **stream:** a very small river
- ⓘ **swimmin' hole:** a small area of water where local people like to go . . . *swimming*!
- **tent:** a small shelter for sleeping outside; made from a strong material
- **territory:** an area of land
- **unlimited:** no limit! have as much of something as you want
- **view:** a beautiful scene
- **Western** (movie): a type of movie about life in the "wild wild west," with cowboys, and horses, and good guys and bad guys. Yee haw!
- **white water:** a river that moves very, very fast over rocks; the water looks white in those rocky places
- **whitewater rafting:** floating down rivers that move very, very fast over rocks
- ⓘ **yummy:** delicious!

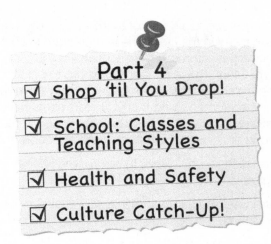

SHOP 'TIL YOU DROP!

Well, we have to say it: you guys are very, very smart. You came up with an excellent plan: *"Hey, here's a great idea—why don't we pretend we want to go to college in the U.S.? Then we can spend lots of time* SHOPPING!" Haha—we're just kidding! We know you came here to study, work hard, and learn everything you can about American culture. We also know that one of your favorite parts of American culture is . . . SHOPPING! (Okay, we admit it. It's one of *our* favorite parts too, ha.)

We're not talking about grocery shopping. We're talking about . . . THE MALL!

Like big shopping malls everywhere, American malls are designed to make people want to spend lots of time there. We think you can figure out why. Spend *time* . . . spend *money*! Just think about it—the **department stores**! The designer **boutiques**! The cool **home furnishings** stores! The electronics **kiosks**! The fancy chocolate shops with *free samples*! And . . . yes, you know what we love . . . **THE FOOD COURT!** So many things to buy—and so many places to buy things!

We think some genius must have figured out how to design shopping malls, because there's something for everyone, everywhere you go. Big malls are divided into sections. Sometimes they're marked by colors, or cute names; sometimes the areas are just known by a very large, very popular store in the section. (You may recognize some of them—many big international stores are very successful in the U.S.) These stores are known as **anchor stores**. They're the largest stores in their sections of the mall, with many little shops around them. Often, these anchor stores are traditional department stores. (We call them *department stores* because they have many . . . well . . . *departments!*) The Women's and Men's Departments have clothes from different **designers**, as well as **moderately** priced items. The Shoe Department has tons of . . . um . . . shoes! There are departments for:

- Housewares: dishes, cookware, things for the kitchen and for entertaining guests

- Furniture and Bedding: lamps, tables, and chairs; blankets, sheets, pillows, and linens

- Cosmetics: makeup and perfume with plenty of free samples!

- Giftware: pretty things for special people (hey—you can buy a gift for yourself too!)

- Accessories: belts, hats, scarves, bags, and jewelry

We know—that sounds like an entire mall in one store, doesn't it? Yes, department stores are pretty big, and they usually have at least two or three **floors**. To help you move easily from floor to floor, **escalators** are located in a central part of the store. **Elevators** may be a little harder to find—they are usually in a corner of the store. **Restrooms** are usually near the Customer Service area, often on a top floor. You may be thinking it can be tricky finding what you want. No problem! There are signs posted near the escalators that show what items you can find on each level.

The signs in each store help you know where you can find the things you're shopping for, but some shopping malls are so big, with so many stores, and so many sections, that you may think about turning on your **GPS** so you don't get lost! That would work, or you could just pick up a mall map at the Customer Service area. And, if you lose the map in one of your shopping bags, you can just check the mall **directory**. These are located in each section of the mall, and they show you where you are now (YOU ARE HERE!), and where all of the stores in the section are located. But it's a good idea to pick up an information brochure at Customer Service. It will have a map of the stores and all kinds of helpful information: mall hours, special opening and closing times for holidays, **events** at the mall, a listing of the stores, and (most important to us)—where to find the food court! The food court is a large central area with tables. All around this space are fast food restaurants serving just about anything you're hungry for: pizza, sandwiches, cheeseburgers, salads, all types of ethnic foods . . . we're getting hungry just thinking about it! All your friends can choose something different, and everyone can sit together in the main table area.

Many malls have sit-down chain restaurants too, so after a busy day of shopping, you can go into a restaurant, order from a menu, and relax. In fact, lots of people go to the mall just to eat at the restaurants. For those people, the restaurants often have **valet parking**. You can drive your car right up to the outside door where a valet will take your keys and park the car for you. You head inside to a very nice table for a very nice meal. Valet parking is usually free, but you are always expected to tip the valet when he returns the car.

Besides shopping and eating, there are lots of things to do at the mall. While your friend gets a haircut at the **salon**, you can get **pampered** and have a **mani-pedi**. Then grab a snack before you see a movie. Kiosks throughout the mall offer sunglasses, phones, soaps, **personalized** gifts, and special treats at small **stands** with just a counter and some shelves. No need to go inside a store—these small kiosks have everything on display, so you can see it all as you walk through the mall.

There are play areas for kids, **arcades** with games to play, and lots of areas with comfortable seating to just relax and do some **people-watching**. Some really big malls are like huge entertainment centers with **mini-golf**, amusement parks, rock wall climbing, and fitness centers. In fact, you can spend a day at the shopping mall without doing any shopping at all!

You can see why the mall is often a place for people to just hang out . . . or visit on vacation. Some visitors actually plan a vacation around visiting the biggest mall in the U.S. It's called The Mall of America, and it's in Minneapolis, Minnesota. This mall even has a museum and an aquarium. Who needs a vacation?!

THINK ABOUT IT

Do you love it? Do you hate it? Some of our best friends would rather go to the dentist than go to the mall, ha! What's your favorite thing to shop for? Do you like to **try on** clothes in the **fitting room** before you buy them? Is wearing **fashionable** clothes important to you, or do you prefer to wear what is comfortable, even if it's not **stylish**? How popular are American fashions in your country? Is American style very different from *your* style? Some people think that because online shopping is so popular, people won't go to stores in shopping malls. Do you agree?

BY THE WAY . . .

Outlet malls are really popular in the U.S. These are often large, outdoor shopping centers with lots of stores together in one (very large) area. But these stores are a little different—they're *outlets*. An *outlet* is a store that sells famous **brand** items at much lower prices. Very fancy and expensive stores and designers have outlets.

People love to shop at the outlets because they can get excellent quality (and fancy brand) things without paying the (very, *very*) high department store prices! But what many people don't know is that outlets usually don't sell the same things that you see in the regular stores. There is a separate group of items made only for the outlets. They may not be quite as fancy as the regular store items. Also, many large stores send their older items to the outlets. You may buy a gorgeous handbag that was made for last year's style. We don't care! If it's a bargain, we'll take it!

LANGUAGE SPOT: EXPRESSIONS WITH *MAKE*

- **(can/can't) make it:** be able to attend an event (or not); accept an invitation (or not); do an activity (or not)

- **make an effort:** do your best at something; try

- **make my day:** My day will be perfect if this happens!

- **make yourself useful:** Do something to help!

- **make a day of it:** spend the entire day doing an activity

- **make a beeline:** go directly somewhere, very, very quickly

- **make a face:** show that you don't like something by looking funny

- **make an impression:** have someone think very well (or badly!) about something/someone

- **make it worth your while:** give something very nice in return for doing something

- **make up your mind:** decide about something

- **make time:** do something even if you are very busy

- **make excuses:** find reasons (even silly ones) not to do something you don't like

TRY IT!

Choose from the expressions above to complete the dialogue below. You may need to change the form of the verb. Answers are on page 234.
Then listen to **Audio Track 11** to hear the complete dialogue.

SHE: Hey, I can't (1) _____. Should I go to the mall on Saturday, or should I stay home and work on my presentation for next week's class?

HE: Why don't you do both? Go to the mall, then (2) _____ in the afternoon for schoolwork.

SHE: Nooooooo! I really wanted to (3) _____—do some shopping, have lunch, do some more shopping, maybe go to a movie . . . HEY! Why don't you come with me?!

HE: Uhhh . . . Umm . . . Uh . . . Well, I'd really like to join you, but, uhh . . . I can't (4) _____ Saturday. I have to . . . umm . . . uhh . . . clean my room Saturday. Yeah, clean my room. . . .

SHE: Ha, you really make me laugh! Every time someone says the word "mall," you (5) _____. And if someone says "cleaning," you (6) _____ for the door. You HATE cleaning!

HE: I know, I know. But really! I'm not just (7) _____ to skip the mall. I really *do* have to clean—my family is coming to visit next week.

SHE: That dorm room is so small you can clean it in an hour. Come with me. I'll (8) _____ and buy you lunch at that Italian restaurant you like.

HE: Well . . . I suppose I could (9) _____ to get the cleaning done before Saturday.

SHE: GREAT! You just (10) _____! It will be so much fun! And I guess I just decided that Saturday is mall day . . . not class presentation day.

YOUR TURN!

What do you remember from the previous sections? Write *True* or *False* for each statement. Answers are on page 234.

1. _____ Kiosks are very large stores that have sections for different items.

2. _____ The levels in a store are called *floors*.

3. _____ Escalators are moving stairs that go from one level to another.

4. _____ Valet parking is for mall workers.

5. _____ Outlets offer very low prices on the same expensive items you can buy in a big department store.

6. _____ Some people plan family vacations around big malls.

7. _____ Anchor stores are large popular stores that attract shoppers to a section of the mall.

8. _____ Your only food choices at the mall are the many fast food places in the food court.

9. _____ Using your phone's GPS is the best way to get around the mall.

10. _____ "Making someone's day" means planning their schedule of activities.

VOCABULARY

- **anchor (store):** a popular store that is the largest in a section of the mall
- **arcade:** an area with video and other electronic games
- **boutique:** a small shop selling very fashionable items
- **brand:** clothing (and other things) made by a special company
- **competitive:** trying to be as good as (or better than) another
- **curbside:** at the edge of a roadway
- **department store:** a very large store, usually part of a chain, that sells many different types of items in different sections
- **designer:** a special person or famous company that makes clothing and other items
- **directory:** a listing of stores (or people) with their locations
- **elevator:** a small room-like compartment that moves people up and down in a building
- **errand:** a small job or task to do (like shopping or going to the bank)
- **escalator:** moving stairs that go from one level to another in a building
- **event:** a special, planned activity
- **fashionable:** stylish; attractive and modern-looking

- **fitting room:** a small area for putting on clothes to see if they look right and if the size is correct
- **floor:** a level of a building; also the base of a room!
- **food court:** A section of a mall with many fast food restaurants, and a large central area with tables.
- **GPS (Global Positioning System):** It tells you where you are and how to get where you want to go!
- **home furnishings:** items to decorate your home and make it comfortable
- **kiosk:** a small open structure in the mall for selling
- ⓘ **mani-pedi (manicure-pedicure):** cosmetic treatment for hands (and fingernails) and feet
- **mini-golf:** a (very) small golf course with fun toys like bridges and tunnels
- **moderate:** not too much
- **outlet:** a store selling things for a company, usually at lower prices
- **pamper:** treat with a lot of special attention and care
- ⓘ **people-watching:** looking at people who go by. It's FUN!
- **personalized:** made special with a name or something special about a person
- **restroom:** bathroom (toilet)
- **salon:** a place where hair stylists and cosmetic artists work their magic!
- **stand:** a small display area
- **stylish:** fashionable; attractive in a modern way
- **try on:** see if it fits and if it looks nice on you!
- **valet parking:** leaving your car (and keys) for a worker to park your car while you enjoy your dinner!

USE YOUR WORDS!

Complete the paragraph below. Choose a word from the vocabulary on the previous pages. You may need to change the form of the word. Answers are on page 235.

Charlotte loves making a day of it at the mall. She adores
(1) _____ clothes, so first she makes a beeline for her favorite
(2) _____. She won't buy just any (3) _____
of clothing; she prefers clothes made by famous (4) _____.
She always makes sure she (5) _____ the clothes in the
(6) _____ to make sure they are not too big or too small. The
best part of her shopping day is finding great stuff on sale! After that she
likes to get her nails done, so she treats herself to a (7) _____.
Then it's time for a haircut at the (8) _____. After all that
work trying on clothes and getting (9) _____, Charlotte gets
pretty hungry. Time to head to the (10) _____. YAY, another
fabulous day at the mall!

SCHOOL: CLASSES AND TEACHING STYLES

Okay, here you are on page 141 . . . How are things going so far? Haha! We'll **bet** you've noticed some pretty interesting differences between school here and school in your home country. And we're not just talking about the cafeteria, ha! Many students have told us that one really big thing they didn't expect is the teaching style of their American professors. Did you expect that all your classes would be in a huge room with 50 other students? Did you think the teacher would stand in front of the room and **lecture** . . . just talk, talk, talk until class ended? Did you think your job would be to sit quietly, listen carefully, and take notes?

SURPRISE! In most U.S. colleges, class sizes in certain subjects are much smaller. In fact, as you get into more and more advanced-level courses in your field, you may find that there are only a few students in your class.

Haha, you better do your **homework**, because you can't hide in the back of the room! College classes in the U.S. are places where the exchange of ideas is considered very important. Most professors encourage (and expect) their students to *think* about and discuss what they're learning. Of course you'll be taking notes and reading about each topic, but your teachers will expect you to express your opinions too. Yes, students are expected to be active participants in the learning process.

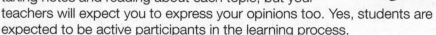

In the U.S., teachers **encourage** and respect their students' opinions. **Speak up**! (It will help with your English too!) No one is **ridiculed** for a "wrong" answer or **view**. Most teachers believe that it is a valuable learning experience for students to express ideas—and **back up** their opinions with facts and information. This process is known as **critical thinking**, and it's a really important **element** of education in the U.S. It means that as you learn information, you're expected to **analyze** it as well—to THINK about it, and to use the information you've analyzed to form ideas about issues.

You won't always see classrooms with rows of quiet students, sitting at desks, listening and writing, as the professor lectures. (*Hey—you in the back—WAKE UP!*)

Now, before you think you'll be going into PERFECT classes, with only six other students, and with professors who have exciting discussions and group projects every day . . . NOT SO FAST! Of course there are other classes that may be very large. Some classes are required for *all* students. You'll need other classes to fulfill your GERs. And of course there are some professors who prefer to lecture, without a lot of student **group-work**. But the most important thing is that *all* professors consider student learning to be the most important responsibility of their job.

In a discussion class, you may be in a room with chairs arranged in small groups. The teacher will expect all students to have completed the reading assignment before coming to class. (Uh-oh! We sure hope you did the homework!) In small groups, the students may discuss the topic, give opinions, and respond to other students' ideas. The professor may assign questions for the group to answer. After a short time, the class may come together and each group will report on their discussion. Some class discussions may become very animated, with lots of students speaking at once. Teachers LOVE for a class to get excited about a topic, but after a time they will expect everyone to analyze and summarize what was learned a bit more quietly.

In a lecture class, the professor may leave time at the end for questions, or encourage questions as she speaks. If you need her to explain something you don't understand, don't call out your question—just raise your hand. The professor will finish her thought, then **call on** you. (Students don't need to stand when they speak or ask a question. Stay right there in that comfy seat!)

Here's an example of how important student opinions are: Just about every college and university in the country has a "course evaluation" process. This is for students to express their opinions about the class, the **material** that was taught, and how well the professor presented the subject. At the end of every course, students will fill out a **survey**. The students will say if they think the **course objectives** have been met, and what activities were most **effective** for helping them learn the **course material**. Did the textbook present the material in an easy-to-understand way? Did the class discussions help you understand what was in the book? Were the teacher's explanations clear? Did the professor lecture too much without allowing enough time for questions?

The course evaluation is an opportunity for students to **voice their opinions** about the class and the instructor, and responses are completely **anonymous**. The purpose of the surveys is to provide information that teachers can use to **design** the best instruction for their students. They may think about using a different textbook, or plan for more discussions. They may plan to encourage more questions. The whole evaluation process is designed to provide students with the best educational experience. So, what do these surveys look like? They usually have a combination of numerical ratings, and **open-ended** questions. For example, typical **rating scale** questions may be:

On a scale of 1–9, with 1 being the lowest, and 9 being the highest, rate the following items:

    1. How well organized was the class? _____

    2. How clearly did the instructor answer your questions? _____

    3. How useful was the instructor's **feedback**? _____

Typical open-ended questions may be:

1. How could this course be improved?

2. What assignments did you find the most helpful? Why?

But that's not all! There's more! In addition to the course evaluation surveys that the college collects, many teachers **require** students to complete a "**personal reflection**" as part of their assignments. This reflection means students must think about what they have learned, and how it has affected them. You may have to analyze how your thinking about a topic has changed (or not!) after class discussions. Have these new ideas and new information **influenced** you? How? How can you **apply** what you've learned to your life? What can you do with this new knowledge? Did you learn anything that makes you want to learn even *more* about that topic? The student reflection shows how important it is in U.S. education for students to THINK about and USE the information they learn in their classes.

Oh hey! One more thing! You may be surprised that most teachers in your college actually enjoy casual conversations and joking with their students. The relationship between teacher and students is more informal in the U.S. than in many other countries. Don't be afraid to talk to your professors. Most will be very interested in talking to you and learning about *your* culture and ideas. These conversations before and after class may be

very casual and fun, but remember that your instructors have **designated** times for office meetings to have longer discussions with students. The instructor probably included her email address in the course syllabus. That's in case you need to contact her about an assignment, or want to make an appointment for an office meeting. Remember that your instructor is a busy person! Don't email just to say "hi" or to be social! Only use email for school questions, and be polite and professional.

THINK ABOUT IT

Are you comfortable speaking up to express your thoughts in class? Is this a different style from schools in your country? Do you think students could possibly have great ideas to add to a class discussion with an expert teacher? We think so! You may find that sharing your ideas will help you to think in new ways about important topics. Speaking your thoughts is a good way to help you analyze and understand complicated ideas. Which reminds us of a phrase that English speakers sometimes use when they don't understand something really, *really* complicated: "**It's all Greek to me**."

LANGUAGE SPOT: PHRASAL VERBS

Some phrasal verbs are *transitive*, which means they must have a direct object. Take a look:

- **call on:** ask someone to answer in class

  The professor called on the student in the back of the room.

  called on → the student

  Call on can't be used alone. It must have a direct object.

Some phrasal verbs are *intransitive*, which means no direct object is necessary. They can stand alone. Take a look:

- **eat out:** have dinner in a restaurant

  When her parents visit her at college, they like to eat out.

  eat out

  Eat out can be used alone. There is no direct object.

If you're not sure, you can check an online dictionary to see how to use these. If you see the words *something* (sth), *someone* (so), or *somebody* (sb) with the phrasal verb, you know it needs a direct object. (HA, but don't forget . . . the way you write or read the sentence will change, depending on whether the phrasal is separable or inseparable.) Some dictionaries will even tell you if the phrasal verb is transitive *(t)* or intransitive *(i)*.

TRANSITIVE OR INTRANSITIVE?

Take a look at these phrasal verbs with *go*. Some are *transitive* and some are *intransitive*. Some are *separable* and some are *inseparable*. Look closely at how they are used in the example sentences.

- **go after** *something (t)*: decide to get something . . . then go get it!

  Lots of people dream of coming to the U.S., but international students are awesome—they go after their dream!

- **go ahead** *(i)*: start doing something. (It can also mean "you go first"!)

  *Papers, papers, papers! Just **go ahead** and start reading them.*

  *The water looks too cold for swimming. You **go ahead**. I'll wait here, ha!*

- **go into** *something (t)*: give details and information about something

    Your friends want to know what you're doing, but you don't want to **go into** *everything in a text.*

- **go off** *(i)*: explode, like fireworks (*YAY!*); make a sound, like an alarm in the morning (*BOO!*)

    Everyone stayed late at the picnic, waiting for the fireworks to **go off**.

    They stayed too late at the picnic—ha, just wait until that alarm **goes off** *in the morning!*

- **go off on** *someone (t)*: speak to someone in a very angry way

    He apologized to his roommate for **going off on** *him about the messy room.*

- **go on** *(i)*: continue; also a phrase of encouragement

    She stopped for a minute to answer a question, and then she **went on** *with the funny story.*

    Go on, *you can do it!*

- **go out** *(i)*: go somewhere socially

    After a long week of studying, it's fun to **go out** *on the weekend.*

- **go out with** *someone (t)*: spend time with someone socially; also, date, as a boyfriend or girlfriend

    They're **going out with** *their school friends on Saturday.*

- **go over** *something (t)*: look at something carefully

    Be sure to **go over** *your papers carefully before you hand them in to the professor.*

- **go without** *something (t)*: not have something

    I'm so hungry; I had to rush to class and **go without** *lunch.*

TRY IT!

Put the pieces of the following sentences in the correct order. Answers are on page 235.

1. about music history/My professor/with the lecture/went on/
    _____

2. to redo/His instructor/his paper/wants him/and go into the subject/in more detail
    _____

3. in the morning/I just hate it/goes off/ when my alarm
    _____

4. because/to go over the application/She wants/very carefully/it's complicated
    _____

5. with your project,/You need/run out of time/to go ahead/or you will
    _____

6. went off on/for forgetting/The rude customer/the waiter/the coffee
    _____

7. so I'll have to/My laptop/go without it/isn't charged/today
    _____

8. as it ran/went after her cat/Sarah/down the street
    _____

9. to go out/The students/after the exam/were happy
    _____

10. another day/I'll have to/If this rain/build a boat/goes on
    _____

Class Discussion

HE: Hey how's your English class going? I know you were a little worried about it.

SHE: I know. I thought it would just be some boring professor lecturing for an hour while we took notes, but it's not like that at all.

HE: What do you mean?

SHE: Well, for our last class, the professor assigned four short stories to read.

HE: FOUR!!!

SHE: Well, yes and no. There were four stories, but she divided the class into **four groups of four** students. Each group had to read one of the stories for homework.

HE: And?

SHE: In class we got into our groups to talk about the story. We had discussion questions to **guide** us. Being in a small group made it really easy for me to add my two cents.

HE: What were the stories about?

SHE: That's what was so interesting. They were all stories about people from different countries who immigrated to America.

HE: Cool . . . then what?

SHE: Then Dr. Bright moved us into different groups of four. Each person in the new group had read a different story. We all had to **summarize** the story for the others in the group, and then decide, as a group, things like whose life changed the most once they came to America.

HE: Was that it?

SHE: No. After that we came together as a whole class again. The prof went around the groups and asked the **spokesperson** for each group what we had decided in the different **categories**, and we had to **justify** it with evidence from the text.

HE: Did all the groups agree?

SHE: No, that was the cool part. One group really disagreed with my group and it turned out to be quite a **heated** discussion.

HE: Uh-oh!

SHE: No, not like that! It actually was pretty fun. The only problem is that now I have to write a paper comparing and contrasting the four immigrants' experiences.

HE: Boo!

SHE: Yeah! I guess that's the life of a student.

YOUR TURN!

Based on the previous sections, what seems like a good idea or a bad idea? Write *Good* or *Bad*. Answers are on page 236.

1. Visit your professor during office hours. _____

2. Speak in class. _____

3. Ask questions in class after the homework reading. _____

4. Email your professor just to chat **socially**. _____

5. Be honest in your evaluations. _____

6. Call your professor by their first name. _____

7. Do your homework. _____

8. Use an online dictionary to help you figure out how to use phrasal verbs correctly. _____

9. In a small group discussion only listen to the other students' opinions. _____

10. You should work on a personal reflection with a group. _____

BY THE WAY . . .

Welcome to American higher education! Higher education refers to study after high school, usually at a college or university. Yay, you're a high school graduate! And now, as a college student, you're an undergraduate. No, you're not going backwards. College students are *undergraduates*. Students studying for an advanced degree are *graduate students*. Sometimes the degree system in the U.S. may seem confusing, but we're here to help you figure it out. Take a look:

UNDERGRADUATE DEGREES

- **Associate Degree (2 years)**
  - » A.A. – Associate of Arts
  - » A.S. – Associate of Science
- **Bachelor's Degree (4 years)**
  - » B.A. – Bachelor of Arts
  - » B.S. – Bachelor of Science
  - » B.Ed. – Bachelor of Education
  - » B.B.A. – Bachelor of Business Administration

GRADUATE DEGREES

- **Master's Degree (1–3 years)**
  - » M.A. – Master of Arts
  - » M.S. – Master of Science
  - » M.Ed. – Master of Education
  - » M.B.A. – Master of Business Administration
- **Doctoral Degree (several years)**
  - » Ph.D. – Doctor of Philosophy
  - » Ed.D. – Doctor of Education
  - » M.D. – Doctor of Medicine
  - » J.D. – Juris Doctor (Doctor of Law)

VOCABULARY

- **analyze:** examine closely to discover something
- **anonymous:** not identified with a name; no one knows who said or wrote something
- **apply:** use an idea or something learned

- **back up:** support
- ⓘ **bet:** be sure of something (comes from putting money on a race or game to try to win more money)
- **call on:** ask a student for a response
- **category:** a group of things
- **course material:** the subject(s) a class covers
- **course objectives:** the things you should learn in a class
- **critical thinking:** analyzing situations and information; supporting ideas with evidence and logic
- **descend:** go down
- **design:** plan, create
- **designated:** specially chosen
- **effective:** successful
- **element:** part of a whole
- **encourage:** give confidence; give support
- **feedback:** someone's comments about something (e.g., a student's comment about a class, a customer's comment about a service, or a teacher's comment about a student's work)
- **four groups of four:** four groups with four people in each group
- **group-work:** an assignment designed to be done by a few students working together
- **guide:** direct in a certain way
- **heated:** strongly argued; angry
- **homework:** assignments you do at home. Okay, or in your dorm room or the library . . .
- **influence:** affect
- ⓘ **It's all Greek to me:** I have no idea what you mean! I don't understand this at all!
- **justify:** support a claim or statement with reasons
- **lecture:** (the instructor) talking, and talking, and . . .
- **material:** subject matter
- **open-ended:** needing an explanation
- **personal reflection:** someone's deep thoughts about an experience
- **rank:** level
- **rating scale:** numbers to choose, showing how bad or good something is
- **require:** make something necessary
- **ridicule:** laugh at, not in a nice way

- **socially:** informally; in a casual way
- **speak up:** express your opinions out loud
- **spokesperson:** a representative who speaks for the group
- **summarize:** tell briefly about the main points
- **survey:** questions asking an opinion about a service (like a class!) or thing (like a car)
- **view:** opinion
- **voice an opinion:** say your idea or belief out loud

USE YOUR WORDS!

Unscramble to find the new word from the previous section! Answers are on page 236.

1. The professor gave me some helpful <u>kbefdcea</u> on my presentation. _____

2. I THINK I understand the directions to the city, but I think I'll let my GPS <u>egdiu</u> me, just to be sure! _____

3. There's a <u>eatneddgis</u> lane on the highway for cars with more than three people. _____

4. The instructor <u>gornedcuae</u> my roommate to use her art skills in the project. _____

5. I don't agree with my friend's political <u>ewvis</u>, but our conversations are always friendly. _____

6. The project requires so many <u>teeeslnm</u> that we really need a good outline. _____

7. The survey answers were <u>sunmonoay</u>; no one knew who wrote the funny answer. _____

8. She wasn't sure what career she wanted, but she knew she could be <u>vteeeiffc</u> in the medical field. _____

9. Wow, that was a boring article! It was forty pages, but I can <u>zeramumsi</u> it in one paragraph. _____

10. Ha—I took a class in auto repair. I hope I can <u>pplay</u> my new skills on my old car. _____

HEALTH SERVICES

Another really important resource that you should find right away is the Health Services Center. American universities are **committed** to the health of their students . . . not only physically, but **emotionally** and socially, too. Schools want healthy, happy students! Did you think the Health Services Center is just a place to go if you're not feeling well? . . . *Well*. . . . Sure, the **staff** can help with minor illnesses or **first aid** problems. But that's only part of what they do. Students can get wellness **check-ups** so they *stay* well. People with serious or chronic health conditions can get help managing them at the Health Center. It's also an excellent resource for education programs and information about every **aspect** of adult student health. Do you have questions that you're too uncomfortable to ask a friend? You can talk to the staff at Health Services about *anything*, and everything you discuss is **confidential**. The staff includes (or can **refer** you to) counselors or specialists who can help with mental health issues.

Health Services is a great place to go if you're having a **hard time** getting used to things here. If you feel really unhappy, or if you need some help adjusting socially, or if you're dealing with a really big problem . . . the doctors and counselors at Health Services can help. It's good to know that health information about students is private and protected—the Health Center *cannot* release any health information about you to *anyone* without your permission.

When you visit the Health Center, or any new doctor, of course there's the usual paperwork. You'll need to fill out several forms, including one about your **medical history**. It will ask about any medications you take, and if you have any medical conditions, such as **allergies**. The forms will probably ask you to indicate if family members have any health issues too.

After the paperwork is completed, a nurse will weigh you (*Nooooo!! . . . not the Freshman 15!!*). The nurse will make a note of your **vitals**: blood pressure, heart rate, and temperature, and then you'll see the doctor.

Some universities have large hospitals nearby, and sometimes students think it's convenient to go there for **routine** medical help. Unless it's a serious medical emergency, DON'T DO IT! American hospital ERs are *very* busy and *very* expensive, and insurance can be very complicated. In some cities you might wait hours and hours before a doctor can see you. Unless it's a serious medical emergency, it's always the best idea to contact the Health Services Center on campus. And in a **critical** medical emergency, you should call **9-1-1**! Of course you got all this information at orientation . . . you just have to find it, ha!

Many visits to the Health Services Center on campus are free, although there may be a small **co-pay**. If you need to have medical tests or medications, you will have to pay for those. And that's where insurance comes in! All colleges **offer** student health insurance at a low cost. As an international student you're *required* to have it, unless you're already covered under another U.S. health insurance **plan**. You may be able to choose from different **benefits** plans—**hospitalization**, **ER**, doctor's **visits**, even **prescriptions** for **medicine** that you need. If you get sick, or need any health services, the insurance will cover most of the costs, and the staff will help you **file** a **claim**. Yay! Some plans even offer **dental** coverage, so if you eat too many American chocolate chip cookies, you may have the fun of sitting in a dentist's chair with your mouth wide open, while the dentist **DRILLS** YOUR TEETH! *aaaackkkkk!!!* Nobody wants **cavities**, so let's just forget about the dentist and go eat some broccoli, ha!

SAFETY

We *know* you remember the safety presentations you attended at orientation. Student safety is a top priority of colleges everywhere. You want to feel safe on campus, and your college administration wants you to feel safe too! You may not know that many colleges have their own team of **paramedics**, and their own campus police force. That's right—an entire security staff whose job is to keep the campus a safe place, 24 hours a day.

Of course 9-1-1 is the number to call for serious emergencies. These include fire; a medical emergency where someone is bleeding, **unconscious**, or **struggling** to breathe; or things like a crime **in progress**. But the campus security departments also have a number to contact them directly. If you feel uncomfortable in any situation, or feel that someone nearby could be dangerous, go first to a safe place. Then call campus police. You can do this from any emergency call box (look for the blue lights) on campus, or from your phone. Program the number into your phone!

Have you seen the officers on bikes riding through campus? They're not just getting exercise—they're keeping an eye on things. They're trained to look for anything that looks *off*. And of course they're **alert** to any illegal activity. If you're ever **nervous** or uncomfortable about any situation, the campus police can help.

What about late nights at the library, or coming back from a trip very late at night? Are you nervous about walking alone? Most campuses have a **24/7 escort** service. This means that, **around the clock**, someone is available to escort you from wherever you are on campus to your destination. Simply make a call, any time of day or night.

Speaking of using your phone . . . Be sure to sign up for your school's emergency notification system. This system is designed to tell students if there is any emergency on campus. A phone, text, or email alert will notify students of safety issues in the area, on or off campus. You'll also get weather alerts (dangerous storms . . . snow day?!) that could affect classes or activities on campus.

Your own **common sense** is the best safety **precaution** you can take. Be alert to things around you. If it's late at night and you are unfamiliar with the area, don't travel alone. Whenever possible, stay with a group. Know the area around your university. Know where the blue lights on campus are located. Know what to do in an emergency. Be sure the security and escort service numbers are programmed into your phone. Most colleges are very proud of their security and safety records, but it's important that you know what to do . . . just in case!

THINK ABOUT IT

When you were at home, did you think about what to do in an emergency? Sometimes we don't think about the **what-ifs** until it's too late. How do you think you would react if you, or one of your friends, had a medical problem that needed attention from a doctor? Do you know how to get to the campus Health Services Center? Do you know the process for making an appointment? What's the phone number? Make sure you have all the information you need BEFORE you get sick!

BY THE WAY . . .

You already know to be careful about signing up for online classes. Some online "universities" are not accredited, and your courses may not be recognized. But there are so many types of *real* colleges that it can be confusing. Here's a simple look at the different types of colleges in the U.S.

COMMUNITY AND COUNTY COLLEGES

- These are two-year colleges.
- When you complete your work at a community college or a county college, you will receive an Associate's Degree, or a certificate in a specialized program.
- Community colleges offer many certificate programs for students who want to go directly into the **workforce**, in fields like **culinary arts**, nursing, and security.
- Many community colleges are partners with four-year colleges. This means that you can complete **general ed** courses at the two-year school, and the four-year college partner will accept ALL your course credits. You can simply transfer those credits to the four-year college and continue your studies toward a Bachelor's Degree.
- Many students prefer to begin their studies at a local community college because these schools are *much less* expensive. Most community colleges are public, which means they're supported by local and state taxes. This makes them a real bargain for residents!
- Many community college teachers are adjunct instructors. Often they teach at the college part-time, while also working in their field. They have lots of practical experience to share with students.

FOUR-YEAR COLLEGES

- When you complete your studies at a four-year college, you'll receive a Bachelor's Degree.
- (Okay, sometimes four years may stretch into five years . . . or even more! . . . but usually the degree work can be completed in four years.)
- Although there may be courses in specific trades, students must take a broad range of different courses.
- Some colleges offer an **internship** year, which means that after completing some coursework, students will work and learn at a job in their career field, then complete their studies.

- Four-year colleges are really expensive! The cost of higher education is a continuing issue among Americans . . . and American politicians . . . who want to find ways to bring the costs down. Most students must take out **loans** to pay for their college education, and paying back those loans after graduation is a very big problem for many.

COLLEGE or UNIVERSITY?

In the U.S., any place that you go to study is called a *school*, so colleges, universities, community colleges . . . all are *schools*! There are important differences between community colleges and four-year schools. How about the difference between a college and a university? Easy!

At a college, you will complete studies for a Bachelor's Degree.

A university offers *both* Bachelor's *and* graduate (M.A. and Ph.D., etc.) degrees.

There are *colleges* within universities! Yes, a *college* doesn't have to be a physical place—it is a "school" within the university that emphasizes a particular program of study. Confused? Don't be! It's *all* college!

PUBLIC or PRIVATE?

(This is an easy one!)

- The biggest difference between public and private colleges is that public colleges are supported by money from the state. Ha—so this is where those taxes go! Because they receive state funds, the cost to students is MUCH lower. Students who live in the same state as the college get the best deal—the lowest tuition. If you live in another state, you have to pay "out-of-state" tuition. It's higher than "in-state," but it's still lower than tuition at a private college. International students pay the full out-of-state tuition, although there may be **scholarships** available.

- Private colleges get no money from the state. Their funding comes from student tuition, (money) gifts from people who have graduated, and **donations** from businesses or people who believe in the value of that college. So why would anyone choose a private college? They are usually smaller, so students may feel that they get more personal attention. Sometimes small private colleges have more sources to offer financial aid to students who need help paying for their education.

LANGUAGE SPOT: ILLNESS AND INJURY WORDS

Take a look at the following common words connected with illness and **injury**. Put a check mark by the ones you already know. (Use a dictionary to look up any words you don't know.)

SYMPTOMS

NOUNS Problems sick people have. . .	VERBS Things sick people do . . .	ADJECTIVES How sick people feel . . .
headache	sweat	dizzy
toothache	sneeze	nauseous
stomachache	vomit	sore
fever	shiver	achy
rash	cough	feverish

ILLNESSES and INJURIES

ILLNESSES What sick people have . . .	INJURIES What injured people have . . .
cold	cut
sore throat	bruise
virus	blister
flu	break
bronchitis	fracture

TREATMENTS

MEDICINE What sick people take . . .
aspirin
pill, tablet
capsule
cough syrup
shot

PRODUCT What injured people use . . .
bandage
crutches
stitches
ice pack/heating pad
cast

TRY IT!

Look at the charts on the previous page. In the sentences below, write the word that fits the situation. Answers are on page 237.

1. The feeling when you've eaten too much food. _____

2. You know you're *not* an experienced chef when you're preparing carrots and you do this to your finger. _____

3. Haha, maybe you're getting too old to play soccer all day! This may help your painful knee. _____

4. Yes, there's a vaccine to prevent some illness. Roll up your sleeve to get this. _____

5. Are you having trouble talking? What? WHAT??? We can't hear you! You may have this. _____

6. You've walked all around the city in those uncomfortable new shoes. Your feet hurt, and now you've got this on your toe. _____

7. You're hot! You're cold! You're hot again! Your temperature is 102 degrees. You've got this. _____

8. Who said climbing the big tree on campus was a good idea? You fell, broke your arm, and the doctor put this hard shell on it.

   _____

9. Yes, you really are sick! You feel like the world is spinning, and you need to sit down. You feel this way. _____

10. Oh come on, that's just a little cut. You don't need stitches. You can just put this little bandage on it. _____

Doctor's Office

DOCTOR: Hello. What brings you here today?

STUDENT: I've had a really bad headache for a few days. I thought it might be because I've been studying hard for my exams, but I finished my last test yesterday and the headache won't go away.

DOCTOR: Hmm. Yes, stress could cause a headache, but I see that you have a **temperature** too. Do you have any other symptoms?

STUDENT: Well, my throat feels pretty sore, and it's hard to **swallow.**

DOCTOR: Yes, I can feel your **lymph nodes** are pretty **swollen**. Let's take a look at your throat. Open wide. Say *aaaarrrrrrh. . . .*

STUDENT: *Aaaaaaarrrrrrhhh!*

DOCTOR: Yeah, I can see some white **patches** back there. I'm pretty sure you have **strep** throat.

STUDENT: Oh *ick!*

DOCTOR: Let's take a **swab** to be sure. The results will be pretty quick.

***** *5 minutes later* *****

DOCTOR: Yes, the test is **positive** for strep. I'll write you a prescription for **antibiotics**. They should **kick in** quickly, but it's important to finish ALL the medicine, even if you start to feel better.

STUDENT: Okay, I will. I'll be so glad to feel better.

DOCTOR: You will. And make sure you get plenty of rest, and drink lots of **fluids**.

STUDENT: I think I'll start the *rest* part as soon as I get back to my room! Thanks, Doctor.

YOUR TURN!

How much do you remember from the previous sections? Write *True* or *False*. Answers are on page 237.

1. _____ You go to student health services when you feel sick.

2. _____ The student health center is for your mental as well as physical health.

3. _____ Discussion of your health issues at the Student Health Center is completely confidential.

4. _____ Dial 9-1-1 in a critical medical emergency.

5. _____ A green light indicates where there is an emergency phone.

6. _____ Private colleges are funded by the state.

7. _____ You can complete a BA degree at a community college.

8. _____ At a state university, students staying in a dorm pay only in-state tuition.

9. _____ An internship gives students real-job work experience in their area of study.

10. _____ Everyone has a temperature.

BY THE WAY . . .

Ahh-*ahh—CHOOO*! Have you noticed what happens after that? You may be at the mall, or in the library, or sitting in class when someone sneezes. *Ahh-choo!* There's an automatic response from people all around—even strangers passing by! When someone sneezes, most Americans just **reflexively** say, "Bless you." Why? There are many ideas about that, going way back in history to times of the **bubonic plague**, but few people today really know why we say it. It's just a reflex, something done automatically, and it's considered a polite response. Here's how it goes:

Sneezer: *Ahh-choo!*

Person: Bless you.

Sneezer: Thank you.

Next time someone sneezes, notice what happens. You'll see the exact little conversation above! (As a matter of fact, if no one says, "Bless you," the sneezer may actually feel a little weird for a minute!) By the way, it's considered polite to sneeze into a tissue, or into your elbow. No one wants to catch your cold!

VOCABULARY

- ⓘ **24/7:** 24 hours a day, 7 days a week . . . ALWAYS!
- **9-1-1:** emergency phone number
- **alert:** being watchful
- **allergy:** a reaction to something, like a medication, a plant substance, or a food, that causes discomfort or medical symptoms
- **antibiotics:** medicines to kill microorganisms like bacteria that cause infection
- ⓘ **around the clock:** 24/7, 24 hours a day, 7 days a week . . . ALWAYS!
- **aspect:** part; characteristic
- **benefit** (medical)**:** money paid by a company for medical expenses
- **bubonic plague:** a disease that spreads easily from person to person, and that usually causes death. (It's very uncommon today, but during times in history it was a terrible problem in many countries.)
- **cavity:** a space or a hole, especially in a tooth
- ⓘ **check-up:** a visit to a doctor, just to be sure everything is still fine!

- **claim:** a request for payment
- **co-pay:** money you have to pay when you see the doctor or get some medicine. Amount varies depending on your medical insurance plan.
- **commit:** really want to do something and decide to do it!
- **common sense:** practical knowledge
- **confidential:** completely private
- **critical:** extremely serious
- **culinary arts:** all about FOOD and cooking. Sign us up!
- **dental:** having to do with teeth
- **donations:** money given to support a good cause
- **drill:** use that dental tool to fix a tooth. You know the one we mean: ZZZZZZZZZZZzzzzzzzzzzzzzz!!! Ugh! NNNnoooooo!!!!
- **emotionally:** having to do with feelings
- **ER:** Emergency Room
- **escort:** going with someone to a place, or the person who goes with you
- **file:** enter, send, or save a form
- **first aid:** medical help given to someone until professional help is available
- **fluids:** liquids
- ⓘ **general ed:** general education requirements, GERs, classes you HAVE to take to graduate
- ⓘ **hard time:** difficulty, either physically or emotionally
- **hospitalization:** an insurance plan to cover expenses if you need to be in the hospital
- **in progress:** going on now! Something started, but not finished.
- **injury:** hurt; damage done to the body
- **internship:** a temporary job to get training in the workplace (You get great experience, but probably no money!)
- ⓘ **kick in:** have an effect; start to work
- **lymph nodes:** things in the body medical people know stuff about!
- **medical history:** list of past and present medical issues

- **medicine:** something you take to cure an illness
- **nervous:** anxious, not relaxed; worried
- ⓘ **off:** strange, unusual; not as it should be
- **offer:** provide; make something available
- **paramedic:** emergency responder
- **patches:** areas or sections
- **positive:** yes, you have the condition!
- **plan:** arrangement
- **precaution:** something you do to try to prevent a problem
- **prescription:** paper the doctor gives you saying what medicine the pharmacist needs to give you
- **refer:** send to another person who knows more about the issue
- **reflexively:** without thinking; automatically
- **routine:** usual, common; everyday
- **scholarship:** money given to a student who meets certain qualifications, to help pay for their education
- **staff:** employees (non-teaching in a college)
- **strep:** a bacterial infection of the throat
- **struggle:** have difficulty
- **swab:** use a piece of material to get a sample from the mouth to test for bacteria
- **swallow:** have food or liquid go down the throat
- **swollen:** larger than normal, often because of illness or injury
- **symptom:** a sign of an illness
- a **temperature:** body temperature (heat) above normal; a fever; a symptom of illness
- **unconscious:** breathing, but not responding
- **visit:** time spent at a doctor's office
- ⓘ **vitals:** temperature, heart rate, blood pressure
- ⓘ **what-ifs:** what could possibly happen
- **workforce:** people in a job

USE YOUR WORDS!

Circle the correct word in the sentences below. Answers are on page 238.

1. The student was lucky to get a/an *(scholarship/internship)* working at a company in the city.

2. It's *(common sense/off)* to stay with a group when walking at night in a strange place.

3. The instructor's *(routine/precaution)* plan included taking attendance at the start of class.

4. The Student Health Center is a great resource for students going through (a *hard time/bubonic plague*).

5. A *(benefit/co-pay)* is money you may have to pay to see a doctor.

6. Campuses will always provide a/an *(visit/escort)* if you are uncomfortable walking anywhere on campus.

7. *(Confidential/General ed)* information will not be shared with anyone.

8. The number to call in a serious emergency is *(24-7/9-1-1)*.

9. A temperature is a *(critical/symptom)* of an illness.

10. A person's medical *(history/prescription)* is a list of past and present illnesses.

FUN WITH IDIOMATIC EXPRESSIONS: Sick!

- **sick as a dog:** really, *really* not feeling well
  *I really wanted to go to that baseball game in Baltimore, but I was as **sick as a dog** and couldn't make it.*

- **feel sick to your stomach:** be so upset by something that you almost feel physically ill
  *When they told her she missed the **deadline** by one day, and she lost her chance to apply for a visa, she felt **sick to her stomach**.*

- **sick (to death)** of something: really annoyed and tired of something that's been going on
  *He was **sick to death** of his roommate smoking in the bathroom, so he decided to change rooms.*

- **sick and tired:** annoyed by something that's been going on
  *The whole class was **sick and tired** of the student always interrupting the professor.*

- **makes me sick:** really upsets me
  *It **makes me sick** to see those students leaving their trash on the park bench.*

- **worried sick:** very, *very* concerned about something
  *Your mom will be **worried sick** if you don't call to let her know you arrived safely.*

- **call in/out sick:** tell people at school or work that you won't be coming in because you don't feel well
  *Class was canceled because Professor Gilmore **called out sick**.*

- **sick in bed:** so ill that you stay in bed
  *It's a good thing I didn't try to go to Baltimore. I was **sick in bed** for two days!*

- **sick day:** a day when you don't go to work or school. Some businesses offer a number of sick days that a worker is allowed to take without losing pay.
  *I've been sneezing all day, and I feel achy and nauseous. I think I need to take a **sick day** today.*

- **sick** (slang): crazy, cool, awesome!
  *Dude, that awesome new skateboard is **sick**!*

TRY IT!

Add the best expression to complete the sentences below. Answers are on page 238.

1. He was so nervous about the presentation to the faculty committee that he felt _____.

2. I'm really _____ of this weather. It's been raining for two weeks straight.

3. I've been _____ about my little pooch. Does he miss me?

4. I was supposed to work at the coffee shop today, but I think I'm getting the flu. I'll have to _____.

5. He must be _____ if he's not at the game. He hasn't missed a soccer game since the season started.

JUST FOR FUN!

Here's our favorite doctor joke:

Patient: Doctor, my eye hurts when I drink my cup of coffee.

Doctor: Hmm. Okay, tomorrow remember to take the spoon out before you drink it.

TIP: Old School

There's a pretty popular expression used quite commonly in American slang. It's the phrase *old school*. If something is *old school*, it's the old way of doing things. Handing in printed papers is *old school* in many places because students today commonly submit assignments online. Handing in handwritten papers is really *old school*! Using a camera is *old school*, because so many people use their smartphones to take pictures. You get the idea!

TIP: 9-1-1

Here's the most important number you need to know: 9-1-1. It's the number that's used throughout the U.S. for emergencies. For a medical emergency—call 9-1-1. For a police emergency—call 9-1-1. For a fire emergency—call 9-1-1. You get the idea—9-1-1 is the number to remember for any serious emergency.

Most states have a law requiring drivers to **pull over** to the side of the road when they hear an emergency vehicle. All cars should stop—yes, even if the traffic light is green—until emergency vehicles have passed. Those vehicles have a very serious job to do—let them get there quickly!

ROAD TRIP: Disney World in Orlando, Florida

Are you a **thrill seeker**? Want to **spin** around, **flip** upside-down, turn *this way* and *that way*, go up and down, go left and right, plus see the latest in 3D technology? Then you can't spend four years in the U.S. without going here! Orlando, Florida means a ton of theme parks, and theme parks mean **rides**! You only have to say "Disney" to think: magic. Do you like Harry Potter? Universal is the place for you. Are you more of an animal person? Try SeaWorld and Animal Kingdom.

Here are our top tips for the parks:

What to Bring:

- Patience!
- Sunscreen
- Comfortable shoes (You'll do lots of walking.)
- A towel and dry clothes for the water rides

How to Enjoy More Rides:

- Buy an express pass or a fast pass.
- Go in the single rider line. You won't get to sit with your friend but the line moves much faster.

Okay, yes—these parks are very expensive, especially for students trying to keep an eye on their spending. It's a pricey vacation, but there are ways to pinch pennies:

- Check out the ticket deals online. You can get combination tickets that may be cheaper.
- If you're not too far away, drive with a friend and share costs. It's cheaper than flying. Bring singles and quarters to pay the **tolls** on the roads.

- If you travel in a group, look for hotel rooms that have extra beds available.

- Look for a hotel room with a kitchen area so you don't have to eat out for every meal.

- Think about one of the home-sharing services! People all over the world rent out rooms, entire apartments, or their houses. Search for apps, or find them on the Internet. You can get a great deal. Cool!

- You're not allowed to bring food or drinks into the parks. If you buy a special **souvenir** cup, you're allowed to have free refills all day. You'll need them—it's HOT in Orlando, Florida!

☑ QUICK FACTS

☑ States have different driving laws, so if you're taking a road trip, read the signs and obey the state's rules! For example, highway speed limits may change as you go from one state to another.

☑ Most places (except for big cities, like NYC) allow cars to make a right turn when the traffic light is red, if the driver sees that no cars are coming. But watch for signs that say NO TURN ON RED.

☑ New Jersey roads are famous (and not in a good way!) for their **jughandles.** To make a left turn on many NJ roads, you must make a right turn. WHAT??!! We're not kidding! Signs will say, "All turns from right lane." Once you exit to the right, the road will **loop** around to a traffic light where you can make the left turn more safely. And it can be a pretty long loop! Welcome to New Jersey!

☑ You may be familiar with *roundabouts*, which we often call *traffic circles*. Drivers must **yield** to traffic when they enter the circle.

☑ WATCH OUT for **pedestrians**! Most places have a law giving the **right of way** to pedestrians in a **crosswalk**. Remember that as soon as you park your car, *you'll* be a pedestrian too!

ANY QUESTIONS?

The healthcare system in the U.S. is sometimes pretty complicated . . . and expensive. Making changes to the system, and to health insurance rules, are important topics to Americans, and people sometimes have very strong opinions about what should (or should not!) be done. Experts (and politicians!) keep trying to figure out the best way to keep a healthcare system affordable, without losing the excellent quality Americans expect.

Medicare is a federal government health insurance program for people who are 65 and older, and for some other groups with special needs.

Medicaid is a government healthcare program for people with very low incomes who could not pay for healthcare without this assistance.

VOCABULARY

- **crosswalk:** a designated place on a road for walkers to move to the other side of the road
- **deadline:** the latest time that something must be completed, or it will not be accepted
- **flip:** turn over quickly . . . really quickly!
- **jughandle:** HAHAHA! It's a system for turning on roads in New Jersey. The formation LOOKS like the handle of a jug (container). You have to turn RIGHT to go LEFT!!! That's NJ for you!
- **loop:** a curving formation; kind of circular
- **pedestrian:** person walking
- **pull over:** move your car to the side of the road
- **rides:** those "FUN" adventure activities that flip you and spin you
- **right of way:** you can go first
- **souvenir:** something purchased to remind you of a special visit
- **spin:** turn around really quickly
- **thrill seeker:** someone looking for an exciting time
- **toll:** a charge for using some roads; these usually require cash payments
- **yield:** allow someone else to go first

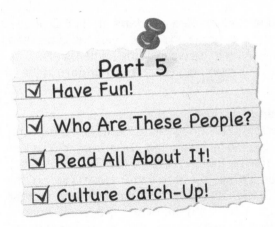

Part 5

- ☑ Have Fun!
- ☑ Who Are These People?
- ☑ Read All About It!
- ☑ Culture Catch-Up!

HAVE FUN!

Yes, we know. You came here to have an excellent academic experience. You came here to study. You came here to work hard. You came here to learn about American culture. Well, we're very happy to tell you that a big part of that culture is . . . to HAVE FUN! Remember what we said about joining activities and clubs: "Work hard. PLAY hard!" You may already have noticed one of the most important ways of having fun on campus: football!

ARE YOU READY FOR SOME FOOTBALL?

Okay, we have to admit it: We're not **crazy about** sports. Our favorite sport is sitting in a comfy chair, with a snack, reading a book! (Yes, we know that just about everyone else in the U.S. *is* crazy about sports.) We may not know all the rules, but we know this: College sports teams are hugely popular, and the most popular sport is football. (No, not *soccer* . . . we're talking about *American* football.) Ask anyone during the football season, "Hey, what are you doing this weekend?" We can tell you the answer will probably be, "I'm going to the game!" Even non-sports people like us get in on the fun.

Picture this: a huge stadium filled with **fans**. It's LOUD. It seems to be a sea of orange . . . or red . . . or green and gray! Everyone is dressed in the team's colors. Everyone seems to be wearing the same t-shirt . . . or **hoodie** . . . or jacket. People are waving big crazy **foam fingers** in the air ("We're Number 1!")!

People are wearing silly hats! People have their faces painted in two colors! YES, their *FACES ARE PAINTED*! And everywhere, people are laughing and **cheering**. "YAY!! GO TIGERS!" Okay, maybe there's a loud "*NOOOOOO . . .*" if their team misses a **play**, but even if their team is losing, the fans CHEER "*GOOOOOO, TEAM!!!!!*" Yes, a college football game is an *event* . . . but it's more of an *experience*. And yes, everyone wants to get in on the action: students, their families; faculty, *their* families; alumni, *their families;* people in the community, *their families* . . . you get the idea. College football is for EVERYONE!

Hmm, but here's the problem with that: Everyone wants tickets to the game! Sometimes, in large schools with winning teams, getting tickets to the game can be tricky . . . and expensive! Students are usually given first preference for buying tickets, but alumni and people in the community often buy **season tickets, year after year**. With a season ticket, fans can attend every game, and they have the same seats every time.

But the fun doesn't start at the game. It starts when you get dressed! Wearing team clothes is very popular, and most people will have at least one t-shirt with the school's name. Lots of people like to wear a team **jersey** on **Game Day** . . . or with jeans and casual clothes every day! A jersey is a shirt just like the one that players wear, with a big number on it. Some people even have the jersey personalized with their own name, or with the name of their favorite player. Whatever you wear, just be sure you're wearing the school colors! And if you're wondering where you can get all this college and team stuff, just head over to the college bookstore. They've got it all— clothes, mugs, **banners**, foam #1 fingers! All the crazy stuff you need to be the perfect fan is right there!

Okay, you're wearing your school t-shirt. You've got your ticket for the game. You're ready to cheer for your team. Then it's time for . . .

TAILGATING!

Can you guess why this is one of our favorites? Ha, it involves FOOD! Tailgating is a Game Day tradition. It's a big party in the parking lot. Yes, in the PARKING LOT! Groups of people stand around the backs of their cars or trucks, eating and drinking. People set up grills and cook the usual barbecue foods: hot dogs, hamburgers, and chicken. Some fans like to show off their cooking skills by making fancy foods. Some even have **cook-offs**—contests to see who can make the best food. (Ha, that's a contest we will *never* win!) Depending on where you live, special foods will vary. For example, **barbecue** is really popular in the South. Philadelphia is famous for **cheesesteaks**. We're not sure about this, but we've always wondered if they serve salad at tailgate parties in California, ha! Hey, California people—tell us! Friends bring something to share: potato salad, **corn on the cob**, mac and cheese, pretzels, and chips . . . you get the idea. Food! FUN!

When game time arrives, the fun moves inside. And the first thing to happen, as with all big sporting events in the U.S., is singing the national anthem. After that, it's GAME ON! Fans get really excited—cheering and **chanting** to support their team. We told you it was loud!

MASCOTS AND CHEERING!

So who starts all this **yelling** and cheering and chanting? Those crazy team **mascots**! Think about the team names: they're usually symbols of strength and power. There are Tigers, Bulldogs, Bears, and Gators (← for *alligators*— bonus points if you can you guess what team the *Gators* represent! . . . Okay, keep reading; we'll tell you . . .)

The mascots are wacky characters dressed in team colors to represent the team. And yes, (here comes the answer . . .) the *University of Florida* team mascot is a giant *alligator* because the team players are called the UF *Gators*!

The mascots are really fun for everyone. Their job is to do silly things—**pose** for pictures, entertain the fans, and get everyone excited and cheering. The chants are easy, fun . . . and funny!

Here are some of our favorites:

- Virginia Tech: Fans on one side of the stadium yell: "Let's GO!" Then the other side of the stadium answers, "HO-KIES!" Repeat! (Don't ask what a Hokie is . . . it's a long story. Just know that Hokies are Virginia Tech fans!)

- The University of Georgia's mascot is a bulldog. Their chant makes us laugh every time! "*GOOOOOOOOOO* **DAWGS**! **Sic 'em!** *woof woof woof woof woof. . . .*"

- In Seattle, the University of Washington fans are also "dawgs!" Their chant is "*GOOOO* HUSKIES!"

- We love Ohio State's chant, because it proves they know how to spell, haha. They chant: "O-H-I-O!"

- Other good spellers are the Clemson University fans in South Carolina. They chant: "C-L-E-M-S-O-----N!" Good job, students!

- At UCLA (University of California, Los Angeles), they can spell AND count! There's a big cheer, then they count **claps**: "ONE-TWO-THREE-FOUR-FIVE-SIX-SEVEN-EIGHT!" Then they spell:

    "**U!** (*clap, clap, clap*) – **C!** (*clap, clap, clap*) – **L!** (*clap, clap, clap*) – **A!** (*clap, clap, clap*)

    U-C-L-A! Fight, Fight, Fight!" (Wow, counting AND spelling! Yay, UCLA!)

YES, THERE ARE OTHER SPORTS!

Believe it or not, football isn't the only **spectator sport** in college. There are plenty of teams that love to have support from fans—men's AND women's sports. Go to a baseball, volleyball, or basketball game. Watch lacrosse. See a tennis match. Try to figure out who's got the **puck** in a hockey game. Cheer as the runners in a track meet **whiz** by. Be amazed by the swim team. Go! Watch! Cheer! Have fun!

NOT-SPORTS FUN!
The Movies

Believe it or not, there are other ways American students have fun, besides going to sporting events. In fact, "dinner and a movie" has been a typical **date** for generations. Because there are so many possibilities for entertainment at home (game systems and **streaming** movies and TV), movie theaters have changed. Now, going to the movies is an experience! **3D** films make you feel as if that monster is reaching out to get . . . Y O U! **IMAX** films make you feel as if you are in the middle of the action.

But even traditional movies in a movie theater make you feel part of the experience. Seats are designed to make you as comfortable as you would be at home. With **stadium seating** and lots of space between the rows, you don't have to worry about someone really tall sitting right in front of you. Many theaters have big, comfortable **recliners**—just try not to **snore** if you fall asleep during the movie, ha! Some theaters even have workers to bring food and drinks right to your seat—now that's what we call service! You're not allowed to bring your own snacks to the movies . . . for a good reason. (Well, it's a good reason to the people who work in the movie business, ha.) The theaters make more money from selling **refreshments** than from selling tickets, so you can see why they're very happy for you to buy lots of snacks. Be prepared for HUGE sizes! (And huge prices!) The typical movie snacks are popcorn ("extra butter" for us, please!) and soda. Enjoy the movie!

MORE FUN

Other typical fun activities are ice skating (usually in winter!), going to the beach (in summer!), going to music concerts, seeing plays, and . . . bowling!

And of course there are . . . PARTIES. If you're not going off campus for something fun to do, you can probably find something fun right down the hall in your dorm. The college hosts parties for lots of occasions, but kids in the dorms get together in rooms or in the lounge for parties too. International students like to prepare traditional foods to share. Some students like to have Game Night—when everyone plays **board games** like **Scrabble** and **Scattergories**.

Off campus there are cafés that host Quiz Night, with prizes! There are silly questions, and questions about all kinds of general topics. There may be questions about music from the 1960s, or about hip-hop stars of today. There may be questions about politics, or about popular TV shows. No googling allowed! If your team can answer the most questions, YOU WIN! These are all great ways to practice your English. Just remember at every party or event: College rules still apply and are strictly enforced. Obey the rules, and have fun!

THINK ABOUT IT

Americans feel it's really important to balance work, study, and play. Is that important to you? Do you feel college students should focus only on their studies, or do you agree that having time for fun is just as important? How do students have fun in your country? Are they as interested in sports as American kids? Do students in your country have as much **leisure time** as American students?

BY THE WAY . . .

You may have noticed that a lot of college and professional sports teams have Native American names. The *Florida State Seminoles*, *Kansas City Chiefs*, and *Cleveland Indians* are examples. This has become a **controversial** subject in the U.S. Some people feel that these names are disrespectful of Native American culture, especially if the team mascots make people laugh at a traditional symbol. Other people feel that the teams use these names respectfully, to show the strength of Native American culture.

LANGUAGE SPOT: EXPRESSIONS WITH *DO*

- **do your best:** try very hard to accomplish something
- **do someone a favor:** be nice by helping someone
- **do a double take:** be so surprised by something that you look again
- **do the trick:** solve the problem; achieve the wanted result
- **do lunch:** go out for lunch with someone
- **do your part/share:** help in a situation by giving a fair amount of work or donations
- **do without:** manage without having something
- **do the dirty work:** do something unpleasant or hard
- **do your own thing:** do what you want to do, even if others disagree
- **do it the hard way:** do something in a more difficult way than it needs to be done
- **do a 180/an about face:** change an opinion to the exact opposite of what it was
- **do the right thing:** make a choice to do a better moral thing (rather than an easier thing)

TRY IT!

Complete the sentences below with expressions that use the word *do*. You may need to change the form of the verb to fit the sentence. Answers are on page 239.

1. Hey, I haven't seen you for such a long time! Let's _____ next week and talk!

2. He found a $20 bill on the floor near the cash register. He could have used it to pay for his coffee, but he_____ and asked if someone dropped it.

3. He left the party without helping to clean up, so his friends _____.

4. Hey, will you _____and return my books when you go to the library?

5. Charlotte planned to jump right into the pool, but she _____ when she felt how cold the water was!

6. He could have downloaded the paper from the cloud, but he _____ and retyped the whole thing.

7. Oh no! There's no milk for my coffee. I guess I'll just have to _____ .

8. She couldn't help prepare before the club's party, so she _____ by staying late to clean up.

9. Websites were loading very slowly on his laptop, so he **rebooted**. That _____ ; everything was back to normal when the laptop restarted.

10. I _____ when I saw Toby's sister. She looks exactly like him, but with longer hair.

Can You Make It?

HE: Wow, I'm glad *that's* over.

SHE: What's over?

HE: My presentation for Economics class. I was so nervous that I thought I might be sick! But it's over. I just did my best, and I survived.

SHE: HA! I'm sure it was great. You're an expert on that topic. Why were you so nervous?

HE: Well, all the other students had pages of **charts**, and lots of numbers, and lots of quotes from experts. I thought that might be a little boring, so I did my own thing and made **cartoons** to show what I was talking about.

SHE: That's BRILLIANT! I bet your presentation was the most interesting of all of them. Using cartoons was a great idea!

HE: Well, I'm just glad it's over. I've been in the art studio and the library for weeks. My friends have probably forgotten what I look like.

SHE: WHAT? That's it . . . we have to celebrate! I'll find out if the lounge in the dorm is available Saturday night. We can have a **potluck**! Everyone can bring something to eat, and hey, I'll even bake a cake! Haha, and you can decorate the room with your economics cartoons. You need to have some fun after all that work. You know what they say: "Work hard. Play hard."

HE: That does sound like fun, but actually I think I'd rather just relax and see a movie this weekend. Why don't you come too? I'll see what's **playing** at the Bridge Theater.

SHE: Hey, that's the one with those HUGE recliner seats, isn't it? I LOVE that theater!

HE: Yes, that's the one. I know—the great part about that theater is that even if you don't like the movie, you can enjoy relaxing in those recliners!

SHE: Okay, let's do it! And how could we forget?! The big game is this Sunday, and we both signed up to bring snacks for the tailgating party.

HE: Perfect! My work is finished, we can go to the movies Friday, prepare food Saturday, and go to the game Sunday. We'll need time to *relax* after this relaxing weekend, ha.

SHE: Yeah, I guess it will be busy, but it will really be fun.

HE: Hmm. Popcorn Friday, snack testing Saturday, and tailgate barbecue Sunday . . . That's what I call a DELICIOUS weekend!

YOUR TURN!

What do you remember from the previous sections? Write *True* or *False* for each statement. Answers are on page 239.

1. _____ The team mascot brings snacks to the team.

2. _____ A jersey is a special team shirt.

3. _____ Before the game, fans sing the team song.

4. _____ Some movie theaters have waiter service for small meals.

5. _____ Football fans think the best part about the game is watching the team mascot.

6. _____ Students with free time should take extra courses to fill all their time.

7. _____ If you don't like sports, there's nothing to do on weekends.

8. _____ If you "do lunch," you prepare a simple meal for friends.

9. _____ Quiz Night means studying together for a test.

10. _____ The most typical movie snack is peanut butter and jelly.

BY THE WAY . . .

Are you a fan of the Harry Potter books and movies? Do you love **comic book** superheroes? Sometimes there's a fun event at movie theaters when they start **showing** a new movie about popular characters. Fans dress up in costumes to look like their favorite characters. It can look like a Harry Potter meeting, or a get-together for hundreds of superheroes. Don't forget to bring your super-power!

VOCABULARY

- **3D:** three-dimensional; not flat—looks like an actual form
- **banner:** a type of flag
- **barbecue:** meat cooked on a grill, usually with a special sauce; also, an outdoor party with food cooked on a grill
- **board game:** a game with pieces moved around, sometimes with questions or cards, usually played on a table
- **cartoon:** very simple, often funny, drawing to show an idea or story
- **chant:** call out repeatedly with a group, in a loud, songlike way
- **chart:** diagram or picture to show information
- **cheer:** shout to encourage a team
- **cheesesteak:** a long roll with steak and melted cheese . . . mmmmmm! Hey Philadelphia? Nice job inventing cheesesteaks!
- **clap:** slap the hands together to make a noise
- **comic book:** small magazine with colorful pictures that tell a story
- **controversial:** causing disagreement among people
- **cook-off:** a cooking contest
- **corn on the cob:** corn, usually covered in butter and salt, and eaten right from the cob
- ⓘ **crazy about:** really, *really* like!
- **date:** going out to do an activity with someone, usually a romantic friend
- ⓘ **dawg:** dog!
- ⓘ **'em:** funny way to say *them*
- **fans:** people who really like a team; supporters
- **foam finger:** that big silly glove-like thing that shows you think your team is #1!

- **game day:** the day when the sport contest is played
- **hoodie:** a thick, warm, casual shirt or jacket with a hood that can be pulled to cover the head
- **IMAX:** movies on a big, big, BIG screen
- **jersey:** a special team shirt
- **leisure time:** free time for relaxation
- **mascot:** a silly character that represents a team
- **play:** a strategic move in a sport
- **playing:** showing; on screens at a movie theater
- **potluck:** a party where everyone brings food to share
- **pose:** sit or stand in a special way for a photograph
- **puck:** the small, hard, circular disk used in hockey
- **reboot:** turn a device off, then start it up again
- **recliner:** a comfortable chair that goes back to a lying-down position
- **refreshments:** snacks!
- **Scattergories:** a game where people must write words about a topic
- **Scrabble:** a game where people must form words on a board from letters they hold
- **season ticket:** a ticket that allows you to attend every game a team plays
- **showing:** playing; on screens at a movie theater
- ⓘ **sic 'em:** attack! Go get them!
- **snore:** that loud breathing sound some people make when they're sleeping
- **spectator sport:** a sport that's fun to watch
- **stadium seating:** rows of seats that are raised, making it easy for everyone to see
- **stream:** to play something directly from the Internet
- ⓘ **whiz:** go really, really fast!
- **year after year:** every year, again and again
- **yell:** shout; call out in a very loud way

USE YOUR WORDS!

Match the following words to the best definition. Answers on page 240.

a. a comfortable seat that goes back

b. special shirt representing a team

c. a type of flag

d. sit and smile for the camera

e. love!

f. shout out in a loud voice

g. an activity played with pieces or cards on a table

h. make sounds with your hands

i. a team character

j. causing people to disagree

1. _____ cheer

2. _____ clap

3. _____ mascot

4. _____ banner

5. _____ controversial

6. _____ jersey

7. _____ pose

8. _____ be crazy about

9. _____ recliner

10. _____ board game

WHO ARE THESE PEOPLE?

Ha, did you think it was confusing trying to figure out professor/instructor/teacher? Or college/university/community college? Well, we hope you realize now that they're not so confusing after all . . . and that they're nothing to worry about anyway! There are also some other important people in college life that you may be wondering about. These are not the professors (though we already know how important they are!). We're talking about the **administrators**. Think about it. In any business there are people in charge of certain jobs that keep a company successful. There must be excellent sales people, excellent workers, and excellent managers to **hire** people and figure out the money. People must know about the company and what it does. People within the company must be able to communicate their ideas with managers. Everyone must work together to make the company successful.

You can think of higher education as a very complicated business. For a university to be successful, there must be a lot of experts who can manage the same things that keep a private company successful. In higher education, however, these people must have an excellent understanding of *education* and student learning. Not every college administrator has experience teaching, but *all* administrators must have a respect for the importance of providing an excellent education to students.

PRESIDENT

 We're sure you can probably name the top position in a private company. The person who is in charge of the entire business, who makes decisions affecting every area of the business, and whose main job is making sure the business runs successfully and effectively is . . . the president! And, in college life, that is the main job of the college president. The president plans for the future success of the school, as well as maintaining excellence every day. The president's job is to be a leader for the school—not only on campus, meeting with faculty and students, but in the community as well, meeting with leaders and politicians whose decisions can affect the school. Working with the president toward these goals is the vice-president.

PROVOST

 Another very important leader is the provost. The provost is the administrator in charge of managing the academic **mission** of the university. This means making sure that all offices and departments in the college are providing the best possible quality educational programs. The provost works with faculty and the **heads** of all academic departments to discuss curriculum, and to be sure department needs are being met; they decide what resources are needed to maintain excellence in undergraduate and graduate programs. The vice-provost works with the provost.

DEANS

 Wow! Now this is a job that covers just about everything! The job also varies from university to university, but in general, the ACADEMIC DEAN is the head of a school within the university (for example, the School of Engineering, the School of Arts and Sciences, the School of Business . . .). The academic dean **directs** the faculty in that school, is responsible for the budget, and represents the departments within that school. Deans form relationships with businesses in the community—this helps the college *and* the community. Unlike the other administrators, the dean is almost always a professor. (Being dean is a big job however, so the dean may not do much teaching while he or she is in that job.) The DEAN OF STUDENTS is a different type of dean. This person deals more directly with the students. Deans who work more closely with students **oversee** programs dedicated to helping students succeed. The associate and assistant deans work with the dean.

ACADEMIC OFFICE PEOPLE

 Each department has staff to help students with advising and to recommend academic support when it's needed. Each department has an office and a person in charge who is the ***department head***. Your department is the best place to start if you need help finding an academic advisor, or figuring out how to connect with a learning specialist. These academic offices will also **step in** when a student is having trouble with work or grades. The department office is also the best place to get information about opportunities for students: scholarships, **internships**, research . . . and ways to put what you're learning to use in the community.

OTHER OFFICE PEOPLE

 There are other offices that deal with the social side of student life. In fact, in many places it's called the Office of Student Life! (Ha, we love it when it's easy!) This office oversees just about every student activity in the college. Stop in. There's so much stuff available in the Office of Student Life that you're sure to find helpful information you never even thought about.

And, of course, big business being what it is, there are many, many administration offices. These offices are where you go to pay tuition bills, discuss admissions, get transcripts of your grades and talk about registration issues. It's a big school! It takes a lot of people to run it!

OTHER CAMPUS VIPs

 These are *not* the people with big fancy offices. But take a look around your campus. The administrators didn't plant those beautiful flowers and clean the pretty benches outside where you have your lunch. The office bosses didn't cook that favorite food you love for dinner, and serve it to you with a smile. The managers aren't the ones keeping the building clean, or opening locked doors for you so you can finish printing the paper that's due. There are hundreds of **V**ery **I**mportant **P**eople who help the college stay the comfortable, high quality, beautiful place it is. Smile at them! Say "hi." You're all part of the same great team, making a great school, in a great environment!

HONOR AND CONDUCT CODES

A really big part of college life in the U.S. is the Honor Code at universities. Colleges expect their students to be completely **trustworthy** and . . . well, **honorable**. It's a tradition that the college wants graduates to bring with them beyond the classroom and into their lives and work. The Honor Code is an agreement that the student will not cheat, or steal, or lie about any college business. There are committees of students and others in the college community to deal with any instances where the Honor Code is not respected.

The idea behind the Conduct Code (and the Honor Code!) is that students are expected to bring their sense of **responsibility**, respect, and honesty into their lives outside of school. Colleges are very **diverse** places, with many different people, who come from different backgrounds, and who have different beliefs. Students are *required* to be respectful of everyone, no matter how different they or their beliefs might be. It's a very serious problem if a student does not follow the Honor or Conduct codes.

It's really pretty simple: Be honest and respectful in everything you do.

Here are examples of what NOT to do, so you don't get into trouble:

HONOR CODE <u>DON'TS</u>

- Copy someone else's work (**plagiarize**)
- Cheat on an exam
- Give false information

CONDUCT CODE <u>DON'TS</u>

- Hurt anyone, or make anyone feel afraid or disrespected
- Have alcohol if you are under the age of 21
- Break college rules (for example, no-smoking rules)

THINK ABOUT IT

Students in American colleges are allowed a great deal of freedom. Traditionally, college students here are known to **rally** in support of ideas that they think are important. Students use their freedom of speech to express opinions on important issues of the day—even to express opinions on policies that may be against the college administration. Personal freedom and expression of opinion are basic **rights** for college students, but with that freedom comes responsibility. Are there similar codes of student behavior in your country? Do you feel that student freedoms in the U.S. are valuable to the college, and to society in general? Are college students in the U.S. allowed too much freedom, in your opinion?

BY THE WAY . . .

Sometimes it seems that there is no limit to the amount of information available for a paper you need to write. As you do your research in the library, in books and journals, and on the Internet, there are a few things to remember. First, it's important to **verify** and **confirm** the information *and* the **source**. Just because something is on the Internet does not mean it's true or accurate! Then, when you've found helpful information, and you've made sure of the source, it's important that you use it only to support *your ideas*. It's not okay simply to copy another's ideas or material into your work. That's called *plagiarism*, and it's a serious issue.

There are many ways to use some of the research of others to support your paper, but it's very important to do it ethically. Your professor and the Writing Center can help you figure out how to do this.

LANGUAGE SPOT: PHRASAL VERBS

In earlier sections, we've taken a look at different phrasal verb types. (We LOVE phrasal verbs!) Here are some more that are easy peasy! These are three-word phrasals, and they're easy because the *something* or *someone* ALWAYS goes after the three words. Take a look at these very common three-word phrasal verbs and their definitions.

- **catch up *on*:** do something that you didn't have time to do before (***catch up on*** *homework*)
- **catch up *to*:** go faster so that you get to the same place as someone ahead of you (***catch up to*** *the first runner*)
- **catch up *with*:** talk to someone you haven't seen in a long time and see what they've been doing (***catch up with*** *a good friend*)
- **check up on:** make sure things are okay (***check up on*** *your family at home*)
- **come down with:** get sick with something (***come down with*** *a virus*)
- **come up with:** think of an idea (***come up with*** *a plan to win*)
- **cut down on:** use less of something (***cut down on*** *sugar*)

- **get along with:** have a good relationship (***get along with*** *classmates*)

- **get around to:** find time to do something (***get around to*** *reading a new book*)

- **look forward to:** be excited about something that will happen (***look forward to*** *graduation*)

- **look up to:** admire (***look up to*** *my parents*)

- **make sure of:** be certain that something is correct (***make sure of*** *the concert time*)

- **put up with:** live through something very, very annoying (***put up with*** *the loud music*)

- **run out of:** use all of something until nothing is left (***run out of*** *printer ink*)

- **stand up for:** support; defend (***stand up for*** *a strong belief*)

- **watch/look out for:** be careful; be alert about something (***watch/look out for*** *bicycles on the road*)

TRY IT!

Add the missing word to complete the three-word phrasal verb. Answers are on page 240.

1. Having a dog means there is dog hair all over everything; but I put up _____ it, because he's such a great pooch, and I love him!

2. I really _____ along with my roommate. She has a great sense of humor.

3. My biology professor is a dedicated scientist and teacher; I really look _____ to him. I hope I can be as successful in my career.

4. Everyone in our dorm is looking _____ to spring break. After a week of studying for exams, we're off to Hilton Head for sun and fun!

5. I'm going to the Honor Code Council to _____ up for Tilly. She was accused of cheating on a test, but I know she just asked the other student to borrow a pencil.

6. Driving is tricky in Washington, D.C. There are so many tourists, we really have to watch out _____ people crossing the street.

7. When I visited Angela she was coughing and sneezing. I hope I don't come down _____ the flu!

8. I plan to spend the entire weekend in the library so I can _____ up on my class projects. I'm getting a little behind.

9. I text Alex every day to check up _____ my dog. I miss my little pooch! Ha, oh and I miss Alex too.

10. *Ackkkkk!* I have to _____ a plan to _____ junk food! No more sweets!

DIALOGUE: AUDIO TRACK 15

A Chat With the Dean

DEAN: Hi. Come on in. I understand you want to talk about **withdrawing** from a class, is that right?

STUDENT: Yes. Thanks for meeting with me, Dean Parker. My instructor said I need your approval to drop my Economics class.

DEAN: Well, as you know, the Add/Drop deadline passed two weeks ago, so it's too late to drop a class. What problem are you having?

STUDENT: Oh man, that class is **killing me**! The instructor is great, but the course is much harder than I thought it would be. I'm taking 18 credits this semester, and I'm spending so much time trying to catch up on Econ work that it's starting to affect my other grades.

DEAN: 18 credits is a pretty tough schedule. So you've spoken to the instructor . . . Did she give you any suggestions for catching up with the rest of the class? Tutoring? Study groups?

STUDENT: Yes, I had a tutor for a while, but I'm just spending too much time on Econ. I don't want my other grades to go down, or I'll be trying to catch up on *everything*.

DEAN: You know that if you withdraw from the class it will still show up on your transcript. The grade will be noted as "W."

STUDENT: I'm not sure what that means . . .

DEAN: It means that anyone who reads the transcript will see that you started the class, then withdrew.

STUDENT: Okay, but will it affect my GPA?

DEAN: No, a "W" does not count towards your Grade Point Average. But, of course, you won't get any credits for the class.

STUDENT: Right, I know I won't get credits, but I'm glad it won't affect my GPA. I'm working really hard to graduate with **top** grades.

DEAN: That's a really good attitude. Let's see . . . you're taking 18 credits now, so if you withdraw you'll still have 15 credits. That's important. As long as you still have a full course load, your full-time student status isn't in danger. Okay, here's the form you need to fill out and sign. Then ask your instructor and your academic advisor to sign it, and bring it back to this office.

STUDENT: Great! Thanks a lot for your help, Dean.

DEAN: You're welcome. But do this quickly so you don't run out of time before the withdrawal deadline.

STUDENT: I'll get it filled out right away. Thanks, Dean!

YOUR TURN!

What do you remember from the previous sections? Complete the following statements by writing the best word/s in the spaces. (We've given you the first letter. You're welcome.) Answers are on page 240.

1. People who manage the business part of the university are **a**_____.

2. Like the president, the **p**_____ works to maintain the quality of the university.

3. Your **d**_____ is the best place to ask about classes to take for your major.

4. The Office of Student Life is a great resource to learn about **a**_____ on campus and in the community.

5. The **H**_____ and (6.) **C**_____ are very serious promises to be honest and respectful to all.

7. Although they must respect others' beliefs, students have the **f**_____ to express even unpopular opinions.

8. Student research can include support from other **s**_____, but that information can't be presented as the student's own idea.

9. Information from other material should be checked to be sure it's **a**_____.

10. **W**_____ is the process to exit from a class that is too difficult to manage.

BY THE WAY . . .

Historically, universities everywhere have been places for student **activism**. In the U.S., students on college campuses rally for (and against) causes that are important to them, and to society in general. These include such things as supporting political **candidates** who offer change; but also rallying against certain university policies, or broader issues like human causes or **global warming**. Political candidates in the U.S. often focus on student voters because they are very **vocal** and enthusiastic in their support of issues they believe in. GOOOOOO, students!

VOCABULARY

- **activism:** using action to achieve a particular goal, often political
- **administrator:** a manager of a department
- **candidate:** a person trying for an office or position
- **code:** a set of standards
- **conduct:** behavior
- **confirm:** make sure something is correct
- **department head:** person in charge of managing an academic section of the school
- **direct:** lead
- **diverse:** very different, as people from different places or with different beliefs

- **global warming:** the rise in temperature of the earth
- **head:** leader; boss
- **hire:** give someone a job for pay
- **honor:** celebrate
- **honorable:** showing honesty
- **internship:** period of time to gain work experience (don't expect to get paid!)
- ⓘ **it's killing me:** it's really, *really* difficult for me!
- **mission:** set of goals
- **oversee:** supervise
- **plagiarize:** copy someone else's words or ideas
- **rally:** come together to support a cause; an event in support of some action
- **responsibility:** control over tasks or actions
- **right:** something (like a freedom) that you are entitled to
- **source:** original document
- ⓘ **step in:** intervene
- ⓘ **top:** excellent; the best
- **trustworthy:** honest and dependable
- **verify:** show that something is true
- ⓘ **VIP:** Very Important Person
- **vocal:** saying opinions very strongly
- **withdraw:** drop out of a course after the change deadline, with no credit

USE YOUR WORDS!

Write a word from the vocabulary above that is closest in meaning to the phrases below. Answers are on page 241.

1. campus manager = _____

2. important goals = _____

3. take another's work as your own = _____

4. a group coming together to support a cause = _____

5. exit from a course = _____

6. make certain that something is true = _____

7. a set of rules = _____

8. on-the-job learning in your field of study = _____

9. issue of importance = _____

10. leader = _____

READ ALL ABOUT IT!

The Bookstore

Books - Buy 'em, read 'em, love 'em, recycle 'em! And this, of course, brings us to . . . THE BOOKSTORE! In the old days, bookstores sold . . . well . . . BOOKS. Now? Wow! You can get just about anything you want or need at the College Bookstore. In fact, we think it could be called The College Café/Supermarket/Cool Clothes Place/Candy Store/Gift Shop/Office Supply/Newsstand/Bookstore. What?! Is that too hard to say? Okay, okay, okay . . . let's just call it *The Bookstore*. But you get the idea. You can **stop by** the bookstore in the morning, grab a coffee, and a newspaper (okay, you can read the news on your phone . . . but you still need that coffee!), then head to class. Later you can **swing by** the bookstore café and buy candy and snacks. Try one of their fabulous **to-go** meals. Salad and a croissant? Peanut butter and jelly sandwich on whole wheat bread? How about a **side** of potato chips with that? We'll take the freshly baked giant chocolate chip cookie, please. (Wow. I think we need to go on a diet just *writing* that stuff!) While you're enjoying your latest bookmeal (← haha, that's not a real word, but we think it *should* be one!), you can relax at a table, or in a comfy chair near the window. Read a popular magazine. Use the free Wi-Fi. Check your email. Text your lab partner. Hey, you could even read . . . a BOOK!

Oopsie! Did you **spill** that triple **foam** extra caramel low-fat double-**shot** vanilla **latté** all over your laptop? Not good! (Okay, we **made up** that coffee drink, but the coffee spill is very real, ha!) Guess what—THE BOOKSTORE can come to your **rescue**! Most college bookstores sell all kinds of electronics: computers, **peripherals**, phones, games . . . and many will be able to fix some tech issues. (We hate to tell you that the caramel in the keyboard is probably there forever . . .)

Is the pillow on your bed a little too soft? Do you need a shower caddy to bring your personal items to the shower? How about **hangers** for all those new clothes you just bought? You know where we're going with this: Yes, you can buy all of these things at the bookstore! The bookstore has lots of items that students always need for their dorm rooms. They've thought of everything!

Do you need notebooks for class? The bookstore has tons! Buy gifts for the whole family! Don't forget that sweet little nephew back home—How about a cute little baby hoodie with the school mascot or **logo**? Show off your school pride with the college logo on pens, notebooks, t-shirts, and **workout** clothes. The bookstore is full of jerseys and hats and team fan items to wear at sporting events. You may already have noticed that American students like to wear their college shirts every day as casual wear too. Be college-proud!

Oh, did we almost forget. There's something else you can usually buy at the bookstore . . . umm . . . BOOKS! The bookstore is always well **stocked** with the latest popular **novels**, and a great selection of anything else you might want to read. Of course, you can buy all the **textbooks** you need for class here, and most college bookstores make it really easy to shop for them. Usually it's as simple as going to the bookstore's website and entering the course number of your class. You'll see the books that the professor requires for that class. You usually have a choice: buy a new or **used** book. Of course, the used books will be less expensive. Hey, if you get lucky, they may even have some helpful notes that you can use! (But, ha, don't think you got lucky if there are answers written in the book . . . They could be WRONG answers!)

Order the books that you need online, then just go pick them up when you have time between bookstore café snacks. (Haha.) If you order a book by mistake, or find that you don't need it for your class, the bookstore will allow you to **return** it within a certain amount of time. Don't miss the deadline to return books, or you won't get the money back. And here's a tip: At the end of the semester, the bookstore will "buy back" your textbooks. (They won't pay you very much for them, but the extra cash may cover lunch!) Some bookstores offer **rebates** on textbook sales if you spend a certain amount of money. For example, if you spend $500 on books, you may get a rebate form. Fill out the form, attach the **receipt** for the purchase, and mail it to the address on the form. You'll get a check back in the mail! Yay! Money in the mail!

LIBRARIES

We love libraries! We love the **stacks** and stacks of books, and the quiet-as-a-**whisper** rooms, and the people sitting in cozy spots with books and newspapers . . . Oh, wait. There are people texting and laptops clicking and movies playing! There are computer labs and audio production studios and meeting spaces and art and

historical document exhibitions and recording studios and print/scan/copy machines and **study lounges**. You can **borrow** computers and audio-visual equipment and films and music. Oh yeah, and books. Let's just say this about the university's library: it has everything you can think of . . . plus a lot of stuff that you haven't thought of! And, if you attend a big university, there are probably several libraries. Our university has a library for social sciences and education, a law library, a medical library, a fine arts library, and a communications library. Wow, now that's what we call a lot of library love!

Are there too many libraries to figure out where to go for what you need? Don't forget the library experts who work in each of those places. Librarians are information resource geniuses! They have tons of experience in all aspects of research, and they can show you where to look, how to find what you need, and what you can do with it. Librarians can suggest resources for different projects, and even suggest ideas on how you might present a project. They can direct you to other libraries, or to the right tech resources for **multi-modal** projects. There are so many different aspects to a librarian's job that they are often called media specialists. They can do it all! Many years ago there was a TV commercial with a song about libraries that's still true today: "It's the latest! It's the greatest! It's the LIBRARY!"

THINK ABOUT IT

The library was "the latest" and "the greatest" even before technology became such a huge part of information and research. The library was where university students searched through books, and wrote notes using pencil and paper. Very old school! The methods were different, but the mission was the same: to provide resources, access to information, and services supporting research, learning, and teaching. Take a look around your university library. What resources are available to you that would not have been there twenty years ago? What resources do you use, in or out of the library, that make your work easier? Can you imagine a time when information was not available 24/7, on devices as personal as a cell phone?

BY THE WAY . . .

You will love us for this one! Many colleges are members of a **consortium** of schools. This means that students at any one of the schools can take courses at any of the other **member schools**. Nice! Large university systems have several colleges with different specialties. If you attend the law school, but you're visiting near the medical school, you can use its facilities. Do you want to use the medical school's library? Do you need to use their computer center? Or do you want to wait for a friend in their comfortable study lounge? If the school is part of the same university system, you can just swipe your student ID, and you're in!

And don't forget: At your own college, or at any college you're visiting, if you use a public computer, close all browser windows. Be sure you log out of any devices you've used!

LANGUAGE SPOT: FORMAL AND INFORMAL WORDS

Phrasal verbs and informal language are common and natural in everyday conversation and informal writing. However, in academic writing, professors will expect students to use more formal language. Can you match the more formal verbs to the common phrasal verbs with the same meaning? Answers are on page 241.

a. investigate

b. confuse

c. postpone

d. co-exist

e. examine

f. increase

g. research

h. discover

i. decrease

j. discuss

1. _____ put off

2. _____ go down

3. _____ go up

4. _____ look at

5. _____ get along

6. _____ look into

7. _____ look up

8. _____ mix up

9. _____ talk about

10. _____ find out

TRY IT!

Now choose a phrasal verb or a more formal word for the following sentences. You may need to change the verb form. Answers are on page 242.

1. In American colleges, it's important to _____ ideas in class.

2. The soccer team needs to _____ the match because of the thunderstorm.

3. It's easy to _____ the dates when assignments are due. Make sure you have good time management skills . . . and a good reminder app on your phone!

4. Just like roommates in college, world leaders must _____ to create a better world for everyone.

5. Because of its new programs for international students, the university expects the number of international applications to _____.

6. A committee _____ the kinds of programs that interested students from other countries.

7. Many alumni donated large amounts of money to the college tuition fund, so the costs for new students actually _____ this year.

8. It's important to _____ the results from an experiment to make sure they are accurate.

9. Students in the department _____ work that's been done in other universities to compare and share information.

10. Research helps scientists _____ new ways of using information in their work.

Ask a Librarian!

STUDENT: Hello, I wonder if you can help me?

LIBRARIAN: Of course, what do you need?

STUDENT: I have a **digital story** project to do and I really don't know where to start. I'm not even 100% sure what a digital story is!

LIBRARIAN: Yes, that seems to be a pretty popular assignment right now! Didn't your instructor explain it to you?

STUDENT: Well, yes he did . . . but I didn't really understand it, and I was a bit nervous to ask.

LIBRARIAN: You should never be nervous about asking questions. The instructors here are very **approachable** and always happy to help.

STUDENT: I know I need to speak up more in class. I will start to do that more.

LIBRARIAN: Yes, that's good. Anyway, a digital project just has to do with using computer technology. The simplest kind of digital story, and a good way to start, is to make a movie consisting of photos and a spoken narrative. Some people get fancy and add other types of images, video clips, and even music!

STUDENT: Whoa, let's stick with the simplest one . . . Actually, technology scares the heck out of me!

LIBRARIAN: Don't worry about the technology; you can visit the fine **folks** in the Digital Center on the third floor to help you with that. Anyway, the good thing is that once you learn how to do a digital story, it will be a piece of cake if you have to do it for another class!

STUDENT: That's true!

LIBRARIAN: The most important thing right now is to figure out the content. What's the topic?

STUDENT: Well that's tricky too. I can sort of choose, but it has to be the story of an ordinary person who has done something extraordinary. Not anyone famous. And I just can't think of where to start.

LIBRARIAN: Have you looked at any **databases**?

STUDENT: I'm not really sure how to do that. Can you show me?

LIBRARIAN: Sure. Let's **pull up** the library website and take a look together.

STUDENT: Thank you so much!

LIBRARIAN: No problem at all. I'm happy to help.

YOUR TURN!

Can you answer these questions about the previous sections? Answers are on page 242.

1. Name three services the bookstore provides. _____

2. Do students wear college clothes only on game days?
    _____

3. Must you go into the bookstore to order your books?
    _____

4. What can you do if you buy the wrong book for a class?
    _____

5. Do you have to pay extra for a used book that has answers written in it?
    _____

6. Can you use your ID at other libraries? _____

7. Wow, that's really cool! Can I use any other facilities at another school in the system? _____

8. Many instructors use informal language as they teach in class. So, is it okay to write papers for their classes using informal language?
    _____

9. Is a librarian's main job to organize books into categories on shelves?
    _____

10. Can you find people to help you with the technical side of digital projects in the library? _____

BY THE WAY . . .

Students are still expected to write traditional academic essays and papers, using research, and **citing** sources. However, it's becoming much more common for professors to assign projects that use different types of technology. Very often the projects will require using resources that students might find in the **workplace** after they leave college. You may need to use software that you haven't used before. The professor may require you to create a website, or to show which types of social media would be most effective for your project. Don't panic! If you're not sure about any of the tech issues, just ask the professor or a librarian. They can show you what to do, or tell you where you can go for help. Yay, technology!

VOCABULARY

- **approachable:** friendly and easy to talk to
- **borrow:** take for a time, then return
- **cite:** quote words or information from another source
- **consortium:** a group that forms a partnership to share resources
- **database:** a collection of categorized information held in a computer
- **digital story:** video of a story using images and sound
- **foam:** lots of white bubbles formed by shaking or stirring
- ⓘ **folks:** people
- **hanger:** something you, yes, hang (or put) your clothes on
- **latté:** a special coffee drink with espresso and milk
- **logo:** the symbol of a company or institution
- ⓘ **make up:** create something not real
- **member school:** one of the partners in a group of schools sharing resources
- **multi-modal:** using several different ways of communication such as words, pictures, sounds, etc.
- **novel:** a story with characters and actions that seem real; a book about the story

- **peripherals:** things related to or used with a device
- **pull up:** find and show on a computer
- **rebate:** a special program of giving money back after buying something
- **receipt:** the paper that shows what you bought, when you bought it, and how much you paid
- **rescue:** save
- **return:** bring back to the store for a refund of your money
- **shot:** in coffee, a small amount of an added flavor
- ⓘ **side:** a food dish in addition to the main one
- **spill:** accidentally drop some liquid from a container
- **stack:** a pile of items
- **stocked:** filled with a quantity of items
- ⓘ **stop by:** visit casually
- **study lounge:** a comfortable, *quiet* space for study
- ⓘ **swing by:** visit casually
- **textbook:** an academic book used by students for a class
- **to-go:** food taken away to be eaten in another place
- **used:** not new
- **whisper:** speak in a breathy way with a very, very quiet voice
- **workout:** exercise plan
- **workplace:** an office or area where someone does their job

USE YOUR WORDS!

Complete the sentences using a word or phrase from the vocabulary. Answers are on page 243.

1. Hey, I'll be near your dorm this afternoon. Is it okay if I _____ and visit?

2. People all over the world recognize the "golden arches" _____ of McDonald's.

3. This glass of juice is really full—I hope it doesn't _____ when I carry it to the table.

4. My roommate is the BEST! Her desk is always _____ with my favorite candy!

5. Your instructor will have a preferred way to _____ sources in your paper.

6. Sometimes I like to cook, but usually I just get a prepared meal _____.

7. He researched the paper carefully, and he made sure to _____ the author of a helpful article.

8. She really looks forward to her _____ at the gym after a long day of classes.

9. I love my MacBook, but connecting some _____ like a microphone and a scanner can be tricky.

10. What? WHAT? I can't hear you—SPEAK UP! You don't have to _____.

FUN WITH IDIOMATIC EXPRESSIONS – READ THIS!

- **be on the same page:** understand things in the same way
  *Before we start the project, let's make sure we're **on the same page** about what we need to do.*

- **read someone's mind:** know what someone else is thinking
  *YES, I want to go for a snack! I think you **read my mind**! I'm starving!*

- **read between the lines:** understand a meaning that is not stated
  *I know she doesn't like cheeseburgers, so even though she said she'll join us, I **can read between the lines**—I know she'd rather go for pizza.*

- **read someone like a book:** know exactly what someone is thinking or doing even if they don't tell you
  *HA, her mom **reads Charlotte like a book**! Charlotte says she's doing her homework, but her mom KNOWS she's playing computer games.*

- **read the fine print:** read EVERYTHING in an official document, especially the complicated parts about limitations
  *He thought he was buying the bicycle for a great bargain price; then he **read the fine print** that said the tires cost extra!*

- **every trick in the book:** every possible way to get something
  *Charlotte tries **every trick in the book** to stay up late playing those video games!*

- **by the book:** exactly as something should be done, or is usually done
  *Their team decided not to do the project **by the book**; instead of writing a paper, they created characters and dialogue for a short play.*

- **one for the books:** something noteworthy; amazing
  *The play they performed was so different and funny that everyone in the dorm was talking about it. That economics project was **one for the books**!*

- **an open book**: easy to understand or know; having no secrets
  *Her life is **an open book**—she posts every detail on social media!*

- **you can't judge a book by its cover:** you can't know what someone is like simply by how they look
  *He may look like a party animal, but he's really the most serious student I know. **You can't judge a book by its cover.***

TRY IT!

Add the word *read* or *book* to the following sentences. Answers are on page 243.

1. My dog refuses to eat her pill. I've put it in peanut butter, wrapped it in cheese, and mixed it in her dog food. I've tried every trick in the _____ .

2. She's always in the library, always reading, and she has no interest in sports. But when she flew down the hill like an expert on our skiing trip, we knew you can't judge a _____ by its cover.

3. I was looking out the window at the perfect beach weather just as he showed up with sunscreen and a beach umbrella. I guess he could _____ my mind.

4. I can _____ you like a (5.) _____. I KNOW you really want to go to the Italian restaurant, but you're being polite because you know I prefer Japanese food!

JUST FOR FUN!

GAMER GUY'S ROOMMATE: You sure play a lot of video games! Why do you never bring home any schoolbooks?

GAMER GUY: Um, because they are *school*books . . . not *home*books!

TIP: Listen As You Read!

We love **audio books**! We listen to audio books when we commute to school and when we take road trips. We don't go to the gym for workouts, but if we did we'd probably listen to audio books there too! We're sure YOU go to the gym . . . try listening to a popular novel while you work out. Listen to a **biography** while you drive. Listen to a **self-help book** while you lie in the sun on the beach. (It will probably advise you NOT to lie in the sun on the beach . . . ha.) And here's a great language-learning tip: Listen to the book *as you read it*. This will help your reading fluency, your pronunciation and your comprehension. You'll get more practice in the rhythm and phrasing of English. Books— read them, hear them, LOVE THEM!

TIP: Books, Books, and More Books

We love books. We have a huge collection of books. We like having books to look up things. We like to read our books, then place them lovingly on a bookshelf, then look at them and admire them. Then we like to read them again! But we understand that buying textbooks can be tricky. They're often very expensive, and you may only need them for one subject that is a required class—not something you plan to study in depth. If you're on a budget and need to cut down on expenses, there's another way to get expensive textbooks, without making you do without lunch! There are lots of companies that offer textbook rentals—you pay a fee to borrow the book for a time, then return it. (It's kind of like the library; except you have to pay a fee for the time you have the book.) We think it's always a good idea to BUY a book so you have it forever, but if you really need a Plan B to save money, check into book rentals online.

ROAD TRIP: The Last Frontier

Hey, here's a really cool road trip tip . . . Alaska! Alaska is our coolest state—Cool . . . get it? And it's not really a *road* trip adventure, because . . . well, take a look at a map! Alaska is that HUGE state northwest of Canada, and just 55 miles (across water called the Bering Strait) from Russia. If you're in college anywhere in the U.S. south of Canada, you sure don't want to *drive* to Alaska. But if you've saved money during your time here, and you're looking for a unique vacation for spring break or summer vacation, consider visiting "The Last **Frontier**." Alaska may be the largest state, but it's also the one with the fewest people, in small towns very far apart, with very few (or no!) roads to connect them. In fact, the only way to travel among many of the small towns is by small plane. It's a wild, **undeveloped** land with mountains, forests, and plenty of wildlife. Although it is so far north, Alaska does get some mild temperatures, but if you're traveling to the northern part of the state, be prepared to freeze! This is the Arctic, and it is *cooooold*! If there are any polar bears left by the time you get there, this would be the place to see them!

There are many trip organizers in "the **lower 48**" who can help you plan a fabulous trip to Alaska. There are cruises to visit **glaciers**, and train rides

through the wilderness. Be amazed by Denali National Park, home to grizzly bears, moose, and caribou. Be careful if you decide to hike! A good tour organizer can help you plan exactly the adventure you want—backpacking, biking, hiking, snowmobiling; or wildlife viewing and a visit to Denali, the tallest mountain in North America.

We've never been there, but now we think we want to go . . . before all the ice and glaciers melt!

✓ QUICK FACTS

Quick—how many oceans border the U.S.? Did you say two? That's what lots of Americans would say before they really thought about it. But the U.S. is bordered by the Atlantic Ocean to the east, the Pacific Ocean to the west, and . . . the Arctic Ocean to the north! Sometimes we kind of forget about poor Alaska, *waaaay* up there! We love the beaches on the Atlantic and the Pacific . . . but, um, we think we'll skip lying on a beach along the Arctic Ocean! *Brrrrrrrrrr!*

No matter where in the U.S. you go, Americans value the personal rights of all citizens. For college students, two very important rights guarantee that they can express themselves on campus and in the community. These are: freedom of **assembly** and freedom of speech. Student (and other) rallies are protected by freedom of assembly. This right allows any group to gather for a cause. At rallies, and anywhere, freedom of speech allows college students (and anyone) to express even unpopular ideas.

ANY QUESTIONS?

- "The Lower 48" refers to the 48 **contiguous** states (states that border each other). Alaska doesn't share a border with any other state (and let's face it—it's pretty far away!). The lower 48 . . . plus Alaska ... that equals 49. So what's the other state? . . . Hawaii. It's our state of beautiful, tropical islands in the Pacific!

- Why is Alaska called "The Last Frontier"? As the U.S. grew and people moved west, land that had been unexplored and wild became home to settlements of people. Development **tamed** these wild lands. The last part of the country to be "tamed" by development is Alaska.

- So how did we end up with a state so far away and so wild? In 1867, Russia decided to sell this big piece of land. The U.S. Secretary of State at the time, William H. Seward, helped write the purchase agreement. Many people at the time thought this was a crazy plan, and the wild place was called "Seward's Folly" (meaning Mr. Seward's crazy idea). The U.S. paid $7.2 million for Alaska. Think about this: Today, one apartment in New York City can sell for $7.2 million! (Of course, the NYC apartment won't come with polar bears . . .)

AND BEFORE YOU KNOW IT . . .

IT'S GRADUATION DAY!

Remember orientation? You started out like this:

Then you studied, worked hard, made friends, had fun, did projects, studied, took tests, wrote papers, studied, had fun, ate new foods, did more projects, studied, visited new places, took tests, wrote more papers, had fun. And after all that, after meeting new people and learning a new culture, after working with new friends and focusing on important goals, you accomplished the dream you decided to go after just a few years ago . . .

You've ended up like . . . THIS!

YOU DID IT!

It's the moment you've waited and worked for: GRADUATION! In **commencement** ceremonies all over the country, students and their families and friends come together to celebrate this accomplishment. But why *commencement*? *Commence* means *to begin*; aren't we celebrating the *end* of all that study? Well, yes, it is the end of those college years, but it's just the *beginning* of the rest of your life. Do you plan to continue your studies for a graduate degree? Will you stay in the U.S.? Travel? Return to your home country? Will you start a new job? It's all exciting! And it's all just *beginning*!

The commencement ceremony itself is typical everywhere. Graduates will dress in **cap and gown**. Faculty, also dressed in their academic robes, will lead the **procession**. Graduates and guests take their seats, and then . . . it's time for speeches. Lots and lots of speeches. Introductions from the college president . . . **keynote** speech . . . **salutatorian** speech . . . **valedictorian** speech . . . presentation of **honorary degrees**. You get the idea . . . lots of speeches.

But you're GRADUATING! So all the speeches are about YOU. The themes are usually congratulations on work well done, focus on the future, meeting challenges, and making a contribution to society. (If you're lucky, some of the speakers will be funny—and the speeches will actually be entertaining!)

The keynote speaker is often someone important or very well known, in politics, the arts, or culture. A graduating student, usually the one with the second-highest grades in the class gives a salutatorian speech, and the student with the highest GPA represents the class and gives the valedictorian speech. Then the speeches are over, and it's the moment everyone has been waiting for! Graduates are called by name; they walk across the stage, shake hands with the president, and accept their degrees. College graduates!

It's a day of many emotions: relief to have completed all that needed to be done, nervousness about what the future holds, sadness about leaving the place and friends you've loved for the past few years . . . but mainly joy and pride . . . in yourself and what you've accomplished. Good for you! Congratulations!

BY THE WAY . . .

It's not "good-bye" when you graduate and go on to your next adventure. The good news is that it's easy to stay connected to the people you've met and the friends you've made—through the magic of technology and social media! **Post** pictures. Post **updates**. Meet up with people who live in nearby cities, or classmates who have jobs in your career field. (This is called **networking**, and it's a great way to share career goals.) And of course, be sure to join the **Alumni Association**. This group plans events and reunions, and shares news of classmates. It's NEVER "good-bye"! Hey, send us a postcard!

GRADUATION DAY TIPS

- Have a lot of **bobby pins** that day to keep your cap (it's called a *mortarboard*) in place. Share the bobby pins and your friends will love you forever.

- Give yourself lots of time. The place will be **packed** and it may be hard to get a parking space. You do NOT want to arrive all hot and sweaty after running a mile from the farthest parking spot on campus. Believe us, we remember that **mad dash**!

- Turn off your cell phone. You do not want it playing that funny tune as you walk across the stage.

- Women, don't wear shoes with high heels! Those steps up to the stage are the perfect place to take a **tumble**.

- If the ceremony is outside, it can get HOT, and it can be long (all those speeches!), so don't forget sunscreen . . . and drink lots of water.

- Try to avoid a bad hair day. You will have HUNDREDS of photos taken and you can be sure they will be on social media everywhere!

BY THE WAY . . .

The *salutatory* speech is a welcome speech, greeting the class and the guests. *Valedictory* is from the Latin meaning, "Say good-bye." We suppose you can say that college itself was kind of like the title of the Beatles' album; it was a *Magical Mystery Tour*, and these two speeches can be **summed up** in the lyric: *"You say goodbye and I say hello . . . Hello hello . . . I don't know why you say goodbye, I say hello."*

VOCABULARY

- **alumni association:** a group of graduated students who stay in contact with events at the college, and with classmates
- **assembly:** people coming together as a group
- **audio book:** a book that is read aloud, often by the author or an actor
- **biography:** the story of someone's life, written by someone else
- **bobby pins:** hair pins
- **cap and gown:** the traditional robe and headwear worn by graduates
- **commencement:** graduation; the beginning of the rest of your life!
- **contiguous:** touching; sharing a border
- **frontier:** border of settled land and wilderness
- **glacier:** a river of ice, moving too slowly for the movement to be seen
- **honorary degree:** usually given to someone for their important accomplishments in life
- **keynote** speech: the main speech about an important theme of the day
- ⓘ **lower 48:** the 48 U.S. states south of Canada
- ⓘ **mad dash:** a crazy rush

- **networking:** making connections with people in an industry, or who share some experience
- ⓘ **packed:** completely full
- **post:** write something, or put a picture online
- **procession:** many people moving in an ordered line
- **salutatorian:** the student who ranks second in a graduating class and gives the salutatorian speech
- **self-help book:** a book that gives advice on how someone can become a better person in some way
- ⓘ **sum up:** give a brief summary
- **tame:** make less wild
- ⓘ **tumble:** fall
- **undeveloped:** not settled
- **update:** the newest information
- **valedictorian:** the student who ranks first in a graduating class and gives the valedictorian speech

ANSWERS
TO
EXERCISES

Part 1 Answers

TRY IT! (Page 4)

1. luggage
2. bags; suitcases
3. bags; suitcases
4. baggage; bags
5. luggage, bags, suitcases
6. suitcase, bag
7. luggage, suitcases, bags
8. bag
9. bag; suitcase
10. luggage; baggage

YOUR TURN! (Page 5)

1. I'm starving!
2. twenty dollars
3. break the twenty
4. two five-dollar bills
5. pack light
6. door-to-door
7. a credit or debit card
8. There's no difference! A taxicab is also called a taxi or a cab.
9. newsstand
10. initials

USE YOUR WORDS! (Page 8)

1. pictured
2. application
3. starving
4. stow

5. shuttle
6. currency
7. stuff
8. crowded
9. luggage
10. degree

TRY IT! (Page 15)
1. Oh no! Rats!
2. Uhh; Hmm; Umm
3. Uh-oh; Oh no; Yikes
4. Uh-uh
5. Wow! Whew!
6. Huh?
7. Uh-huh
8. Hmm
9. Wow; Whew; Phew
10. Man; Wow

YOUR TURN! (Page 17)
1. True.
2. False. There are some sessions that are mandatory for all students; other sessions are not required.
3. False. Some classes are required to fulfill the general education requirements or your professional program requirements.
4. False. You're a student here now! You can use ALL college facilities, but you must show your school ID.
5. True.
6. False. Many will offer a discount, but not all. Make sure to ask!
7. False. It refers to the number of pounds a first year student typically puts on! Eat salad!
8. True.

9. False. These "electives" are open to all students.

10. True.

USE YOUR WORDS! (Page 21)

1. discount
2. venue
3. overwhelmed
4. brunch
5. jet lag
6. mandatory
7. nap
8. flyers
9. tutoring
10. genius

TRY IT! (Page 26)

1. $1.25
2. $45
3. 10¢
4. $50
5. 25¢
6. 25¢
7. 10¢
8. $3.15
9. 75¢
10. $1.50
11. 50¢
12. $1.25
13. $1.50
14. $50
15. $1.00

YOUR TURN! (Page 28)

1. True.

2. False. You pay a credit card bill at the end of the billing period—usually one month.

3. False. The statement balance shows what you owed on the day they sent the bill. The current balance includes all purchases up to the day you checked the account.

4. False. It means you are earning lots of money on any job.

5. True.

6. False. Most restaurants will split the amount among a few credit cards.

7. True.

8. True.

9. False. Some bills show another important American.

10. Haha—TRUE and FALSE! Being *broke* means having no money, so that may make you feel sick! Ha!

USE YOUR WORDS! (Page 31)

1. purchase

2. vending machine

3. transfer

4. PIN

5. change

6. put aside

7. interest

8. statement

9. digit

10. wireless pay

TRY IT! (Page 33)

1. making big bucks/making bank

2. cost a pretty penny

3. adds his two cents

4. a dime a dozen

5. strapped for cash/short of money

Part 2 Answers

TRY IT! (Page 45)

1. plethora

2. vice versa

3. hierarchy

4. paradox

5. alma mater

6. chronological

7. verbatim

8. impromptu

9. ethos

10. genesis

YOUR TURN! (Page 48)

1. True.

2. False. It's common for everyone to be uncomfortable with new foods, places, and customs.

3. False. Culture shock will go away as you make friends and get more comfortable in your new environment.

4. False. Don't be shy! Students are happy for anyone to start the conversation!

5. Um . . . True and false! Of course it's a good idea to join related clubs, but you should also try new things. Experiment!

6. True and false! Usually, fraternities are for guys, but some allow women as members.

7. False. Many people aren't comfortable joining fraternities and sororities.

8. False. You're new students at the same school—that's already something you have in common!

9. True and false! You may find an activity in the community, but you can also start your own group on campus. Have fun!

10. False. Even universities in big cities have opportunities for gardening. Check it out *before* you go. Local communities would LOVE to have your talents!

USE YOUR WORDS! (Page 52)
1. fit in
2. sign up for
3. check out
4. look forward to
5. sleep in
6. stick with
7. Take your time
8. stick together
9. feel like home
10. took the initiative

TRY IT! (Page 58)
1. literal
2. literal
3. idiomatic
4. idiomatic
5. literal
6. idiomatic
7. literal

8. idiomatic

9. idiomatic

10. literal

YOUR TURN! (Page 61)

1. Good idea!

2. Bad idea!

3. Bad idea! Get to know each other online if you can.

4. Bad idea! No matter where you live, you must always be respectful of neighbors. And you should be STUDYING AND NOT PARTYING anyway, ha!

5. Good idea!

6. Good idea!

7. Bad idea! The bathroom is a shared space.

8. Umm . . . Yes, that's a REALLY good idea!

9. Bad idea! Before you go, decide which dorm will make you feel comfortable . . . and request it right away.

10. Good idea! Everyone wants all students to join in activities and be part of the college community.

USE YOUR WORDS! (Page 64)

1. gourmet

2. creative

3. full-time

4. distracting

5. comfy

6. outstanding, exemplary

7. exemplary, outstanding

8. non-traditional

9. dynamic

10. fluffy, comfy

TRY IT! (Page 71)

1. take care of
2. take a walk
3. take care of
4. take a break
5. take notes
6. take a test
7. take your time
8. take a nap
9. take a bite
10. take a hike

YOUR TURN! (Page 72)

1. 6 times: take a walk, take a nap, take a break, take care of (twice), take a bite
2. daily limit
3. minimum balance
4. snail mail
5. little
6. Yes, if you have overdraft protection on the account.
7. The cashier will tell you the card has been declined. Sorry—no purchase today!
8. Yes. You can get cash from any bank's ATM, but you'll have to pay a fee.
9. NO! Schools are required by law to make all courses and activities available . . . and provide accommodations for students who need them.
10. No. Extra time must be allowed only if it's an accommodation for a special needs student. Documentation from Disabilities Services is required.

USE YOUR WORDS! (Page 76)

1. f
2. j
3. g
4. e
5. a
6. b
7. i
8. d
9. c
10. h

TRY IT! (Page 78)

1. started out
2. get rolling/get the ball rolling/get going
3. get going
4. off to a flying start/starting off on the right foot
5. make a fresh start/start from scratch

Part 3 Answers

TRY IT! SIMILES AND METAPHORS (Page 94)

1. cake/metaphor
2. cookie/metaphor
3. cake/simile (*like* having . . .)
4. cake/metaphor
5. candy/simile (*as* easy *as* taking . . .)
6. hotcakes/simile (*like* hotcakes)
7. pie/metaphor

8. cookie / metaphor

9. pie / metaphor

10. candy / simile (*like* a kid . . .)

YOUR TURN! (Page 97)

1. False. If you want that discount, check with the restaurant before you go. Make sure you have your ID!

2. True and False. Some meal plans allow you to use the account at other locations. Learn about the options!

3. True.

4. True.

5. False. You sit down, and a server will take your order and bring your food.

6. False. A veggie plate is usually served before a meal at a restaurant, or as a snack at home.

7. TRUE, TRUE, TRUE, TRUE, TRUE! haha!

8. False. No cooking appliances are allowed in dorm rooms.

9. True.

10. True.

USE YOUR WORDS! (Page 102)

1. i

2. g

3. f

4. h

5. b

6. a

7. c

8. d

9. j

10. e

TRY IT! (Page 108)

1. get away

2. (haha) mess up

3. put away

4. ease up

5. wake up / get away

6. put . . . up *or* put up my sister

7. put . . . off

8. get around

9. get by / get around

10. put . . . away *or* put away the cookies

YOUR TURN! (Page 110)

1. False. There is a short DROP / ADD period of time where you can change your schedule.

2. False. You will have some time to decide what you want to major in.

3. True.

4. False. Each course may have several sections (class meeting times). Check for another section that will fit in your schedule.

5. True.

6. True, if you are an undergraduate. If you are a graduate student, the rules may vary. Be sure you know the requirements of YOUR college.

7. True and false. In some colleges, international students are exempt from this requirement.

8. True.

9. False. Or possibly true! You need to find out in advance what credits the new school will accept.

10. True.

USE YOUR WORDS! (Page 113)

1. hectic
2. snag
3. contact information
4. out of luck
5. show up
6. turned out
7. pain
8. vary
9. pay off
10. keep an eye on

TRY IT! (Page 119)

1. comes and goes
2. over and out
3. off and on
4. dos and don'ts/ins and outs/pros and cons
5. pros and cons
6. ups and downs/pros and cons
7. back and forth
8. back and forth/to and fro
9. rise and shine
10. odds and ends

YOUR TURN! (Page 121)

1. False. You plan your own schedule.
2. True.
3. False. Liberal arts schools believe every student should be educated in a broad range of subjects
4. Haha, true and false! A hybrid *car* runs partly on batteries, and it will save money on gas, but a hybrid *course* is a class that's partly online and partly in-class.

5. True.

6. False. An RA is a specially trained student who can help with your questions about college life.

7. False. It's a great place for help with understanding the new material you're learning in class.

8. False! A scam is a false plan, designed to take your money or your personal information!

9. False. Articles and prepositions are small, but they are very tricky to learn.

10. False. They will help you find problems in your writing that you can improve.

USE YOUR WORDS! (Page 124)

1. party
2. scam
3. ace
4. accomplish
5. easy peasy
6. hybrid
7. highlight
8. loan
9. format
10. in good shape

TRY IT! (Page 126)

1. d
2. a
3. e
4. b
5. c

Part 4 Answers

SHE: Hey, I can't (1) <u>make up my mind</u>. Should I go to the mall on Saturday, or should I stay home and work on my presentation for next week's class?

HE: Why don't you do both? Go to the mall, then (2) <u>make time</u> in the afternoon for schoolwork.

SHE: Nooooooo! I really wanted to (3) <u>make a day of it</u>—do some shopping, have lunch, do some more shopping, maybe go to a movie . . .HEY! Why don't you come with me?!

HE: Uhhh . . . Umm . . . Uh . . . Well, I'd really like to join you, but, uhh . . . I can't (4) <u>make it</u> Saturday. I have to . . . umm . . . uhh . . . clean my room Saturday. Yeah, clean my room . . .

SHE: Ha, you really make me laugh! Every time someone says the word "mall," you (5) <u>make excuses</u> (or <u>make a face</u>). And if someone says "cleaning," you (6) <u>make a beeline</u> for the door. You HATE cleaning!

HE: I know, I know. But really! I'm not just (7) <u>making excuses</u> to skip the mall. I really *do* have to clean—my family is coming to visit next week.

SHE: That dorm room is so small you can clean it in an hour. Come with me. I'll (8) <u>make it worth your while</u> and buy you lunch at that Italian restaurant you like.

HE: Well . . . I suppose I could (9) <u>make time</u> (or <u>make an effort</u>) to get the cleaning done before Saturday.

SHE: GREAT! You just (10) <u>made my day</u>! It will be so much fun! And I guess I just decided that Saturday is mall day . . . not class presentation day.

YOUR TURN! (Page 138)

1. False. They are small places in the mall that sell just one type of item.

2. True.

3. True.

4. False. Most places provide valet parking for people going to restaurants, and sometimes for shoppers.

5. False. Some of the designers may be the same, but the items are often from last season, or they are made only for the outlet stores.

6. True! We can't believe it, but it's true!

7. True.

8. False. Most malls have at least one very nice, sit-down restaurant.

9. Ha, true and false! We think it's a little easier to just pick up a map at the mall!

10. False. It means doing something that makes someone really, really happy.

USE YOUR WORDS! (Page 141)

1. fashionable, stylish

2. boutique

3. brand

4. designers / brands

5. tries on

6. fitting room

7. mani-pedi

8. salon

9. pampered

10. food court

TRY IT! (Page 148)

1. My professor / went on / with the lecture / about music history.

2. His instructor / wants him / to redo / his paper / and go into the subject / in more detail.

3. I just hate it / when my alarm / goes off / in the morning!

4. She wants / to go over the application / very carefully / because / it's complicated.

5. You need / to go ahead / with your project, / or you will / run out of time.

6. The rude customer / went off on / the waiter / for forgetting / the coffee.

7. My laptop / isn't charged / so I'll have to / go without it / today.

8. Sarah / went after her cat / as it ran / down the street.

9. The students / were happy / to go out / after the exam.

10. If this rain / goes on / another day I'll have to / build a boat.

YOUR TURN! (Page 150)

1. Good idea!

2. Good idea! Your professor wants to hear your ideas! Hmm. Unless you're chatting with a friend about the party tonight! Then it's a BAD idea!

3. Good idea! This shows the professor that you're thinking. It will also help to clear up what you're not sure about.

4. Bad idea! Your professors are busy—only email about assignment questions.

5. Good idea! The college wants the best experience possible for students. Teachers and school leaders want to know what is going well, but also what could be improved!

6. Bad idea! Unless they say for you to do that, using a more formal name is polite.

7. Ahem, YES! GOOD IDEA!!

8. Good idea! And online dictionaries let you hear the pronunciation too.

9. Good idea and bad idea! Yes, listen carefully to others, but you should contribute to the discussion by adding your two cents!

10. Bad idea! A personal reflection should be YOU thinking about YOUR ideas and opinions!

USE YOUR WORDS! (Page 153)

1. feedback

2. guide

3. designated

4. encouraged

5. views

6. elements

7. anonymous

8. effective

9. summarize

10. apply

TRY IT! (Page 160)

1. a stomachache

2. cut it

3. an ice pack / heating pad

4. a shot

5. sore throat / strep throat

6. a blister

7. a fever

8. a cast

9. dizzy

10. a bandaid

YOUR TURN! (Page 162)

1. True and False! True: Go when you're sick. False: You should go for wellness checks BEFORE you're sick so you can stay well.

2. True.

3. True.

4. True. Also for a crime or a fire emergency.

5. False. Look for a blue light.

6. False. Public colleges receive state money.

7. False. This is a two-year college where you can get an Associate's Degree and other certificates. Then you must transfer to a four-year school to complete the B.A.

8. False. You must be a permanent resident of the state to qualify.

9. True.

10. True . . . and False! Your temperature is the heat measure of your body—everyone has a heat measure! When speaking of illness, a temperature means a fever—the body temperature is higher than it should be.

USE YOUR WORDS! (Page 166)

1. internship
2. common sense
3. routine
4. a hard time
5. co-pay
6. escort
7. confidential
8. 9-1-1
9. symptom
10. history

TRY IT! (Page 168)

1. sick to his stomach
2. sick and tired / sick to death
3. worried sick
4. call in sick / call out sick
5. sick as a dog

Part 5 Answers

TRY IT! (Page 180)

1. do lunch

2. did the right thing

3. did the dirty work

4. do me a favor

5. did a 180 / did an about face

6. did it the hard way

7. do without

8. did her part / share

9. did the trick

10. did a double take

YOUR TURN! (Page 182)

1. False! The mascot is busy being silly and cheering.

2. True.

3. False. Everyone sings the national anthem.

4. True!

5. Haha, False. Most fans actually like to watch the GAME!

6. False. Some free time is important . . . when work is finished.

7. Oh come on! You know that one is false! There are plenty of activities besides sports. WE should know!

8. False. "Let's do lunch" means, "Let's go out to lunch together."

9. False. It's an event with fun questions about all kinds of topics. And prizes!

10. False! It's POPCORN!

USE YOUR WORDS! (Page 185)

1. f
2. h
3. i
4. c
5. j
6. b
7. d
8. e
9. a
10. g

TRY IT! (Page 192)

1. with
2. get
3. up
4. forward
5. stand
6. for
7. with
8. catch
9. on
10. come up with; cut down on

YOUR TURN! (Page 194)

1. administrators
2. provost
3. department
4. activities
5. Honor Code

6. Conduct Code

7. freedom

8. sources

9. accurate

10. withdrawal / withdrawing

USE YOUR WORDS! (Page 196)

1. administrator

2. mission

3. plagiarize

4. rally

5. withdraw

6. verify / confirm

7. code

8. internship

9. cause

10. head / administrator

LANGUAGE SPOT (Page 201)

1. c

2. i

3. f

4. e

5. d

6. a

7. g

8. b

9. j

10. h

TRY IT! (Page 202)

1. talk about / discuss
2. put off / postpone
3. mix up / confuse
4. get along / co-exist
5. go up / increase
6. looked into / investigated (also, researched)
7. went down / decreased
8. look at / examine
9. look up / research
10. find out / discover

YOUR TURN! (Page 204)

1. Answers will vary: sells books, sells café items, sells clothing and school team items, buys back textbooks, tells you which books you need for courses
2. No, clothes with the college logo are popular for everyday wear.
3. No, you can order them online, then pick them up later.
4. You can return it for a full refund, if you have your receipt and return it within the time limit.
5. Haha, trick question! No, you pay the used book price . . . Hey, maybe the student who wrote those notes failed the class!
6. Yes, you can use all of your university's libraries, as well as libraries at other schools in the system.
7. Yes! Check out the rules for what you can do!
8. No, academic papers should use more formal language.
9. Nooooo, a librarian does WAY more than that. A librarian is an information expert who can help you find resources in many different media.
10. Yes, for many digital projects. And if it's too technical, they'll refer you to a computer pro on campus.

USE YOUR WORDS! (Page 206)

1. swing by / stop by
2. logo
3. spill
4. stocked
5. cite
6. to-go
7. cite
8. workout
9. peripherals
10. whisper

TRY IT! (Page 209)

1. book
2. book
3. read
4. read
5. book

VOCABULARY INDEX

24/7, 163
3D, 183
9-1-1, 163

A

a lot of, 6
a pain, 112
a twenty, 8
abandoned, 49
absence, 111
absolutely, 62
academic probation, 111
access, 49
accommodation, 74
accomplish, 122
accredited, 122
ace, 122
ache, 62
acquire, 131
action group, 49
activism, 195
activist, 49
adaptor, 18
add, 111
administrator, 195
aisle, 98
alert, 163
alien, 49
all over, 49
allergy, 163
alternative, 74
alumni association, 216
amaze, 62
amenity, 18
analyze, 151
anchor (store), 139
anonymous, 151
antibiotics, 163
antlers, 37
appear, 98
application, 6

apply, 151
approachable, 205
arcade, 139
area, 112
around the clock, 163
arrange, 37
articles, 122
arts, 112
aspect, 163
assembly, 216
assistive technology, 74
attentive, 37
attract, 62
audio book, 216
auditorium, 18
avoid, 74
awkward, 122

B

back home, 74
back road, 82
back up, 152
bad boys, 82
bag, 98
baggage compartment, 6
balance, 29, 122
banner, 183
barbecue, 183
bare mattress, 62
bargain, 74
bathrobe, 62
BBQ, 18
bed and bath, 62
bedding, 62
before you know it, 62
bench, 122
benefit (medical), 163
best of both worlds, 122
bet, 152
beverage, 131
billing cycle, 29

route, 82
routine, 165
run out of (something), 75
rush around, 100

S

safety feature, 63
salad, 100
salon, 140
salutatorian, 217
sample, 101
scam, 123
Scattergories, 184
scenic, 82
scheduled, 123
scholarship, 165
scoop, 132
Scrabble, 184
season ticket, 184
seconds, 132
section, 112
see you later, 20
self-checkout, 101
self-help book, 217
semester, 20
seminar, 20
sense of adventure, 51
sensible, 20
server, 30
serving, 132
set up, 30
settle in, 51
shear, 132
sheet, 64
shiny new, 75
shopping list, 101
short and sweet, 75
shot, 206
should, 123
show up, 112
show, 20

showcase, 51
showing, 184
shuttle, 8
shy, 51
sic 'em, 184
side, 206
sign on the dotted line, 8
sign up, 20
sit down with someone, 123
sit-down restaurant, 101
situation, 30
skip, 101
sleep in, 51
slice, 101
slippers, 64
smoke-free, 64
snack tray, 101
snag, 113
snail mail, 75
snail, 75
snore, 184
snow-capped, 132
so long, 20
social event, 51
social, 51
socially, 153
sorority, 51
sounds good to me, 8
sounds good, 51
source, 196
souvenir, 172
speak up, 153
special pricing, 20
specialize, 113
spectator sport, 184
speed limit, 37
spend (money), 30
spend (time), 30
spill, 206
spin, 172
split, 30
splurge, 101

worm, 51
worth, 30
WOW, 8

X

XL, 64

Y

year after year, 184
yell, 184
yield, 172
yum, 21
yummy, 132

Notes